DATE DUE

DE 4'00			
DE 12'01			
DE 3'02			
MY 1 4 '08			

Prescribed Burning in California Wildlands Vegetation Management

Prescribed Burning
in California Wildlands
Vegetation Management

Harold H. Biswell

With a New Foreword by James Agee

University of California Press

Berkeley   Los Angeles   London

University of California Press
Berkeley and Los Angeles, California

University of California Press, Ltd.
London, England

First Paperback Printing 1999

Library of Congress Cataloging-in-Publication Data

Biswell, Harold H. (Harold Hubert)
  Prescribed burning in California wildlands vegetation
management /
  Harold H. Biswell.
    p. cm.
  Includes bibliographies and index.
  ISBN 21945-7 (pbk. : alk. paper)
    1. Prescribed burning—California. 2. Wilderness
areas—California—Management. 3. Wildfires—Califor-
nia. 4. Fire ecology—California. I. Title. II. Title:
Wildlands vegetation management.
S608.B57   1989
639.9—dc19   88-21094
                                           CIP

Printed in the United States of America
1 2 3 4 5 6 7 8 9

Contents

Foreword to the Paperback Edition

The paperback publication of *Prescribed Burning in California Wildlands Vegetation Management* is a welcome smoke signal for those of us in the profession of fire management and ecology. The messages that Harold Biswell sent so effectively began a paradigm shift in fire management thirty years ago in California, but institutional change comes slowly, and these messages need to be repeated.

The man who, more than any other, actually bent the old fire culture was Harold Biswell. The idea of underburning forests to prevent more destructive wildfires was a revolutionary notion in California in the 1950s and 1960s, although fire was routinely used in some shrublands. It's important to keep in mind that during those times Biswell was widely criticized for the same ideas, presented in the same way, for which he received so much favorable response later in his career.

Prescribed Burning, published in hardcover in 1989, is a classic integration of science and interpretation. Harold took a complex problem and presented a complex answer, but he did so in a way that most people can understand. Harold Biswell passed away in 1992 after a half-century-long career of teaching, research, and public outreach, all of which are summarized in this book.

Biswell radically changed the way we think about fire and vegetation, not only in California but throughout the West, and around the world, as Professor Naveh notes in the foreword to the original edition. Radical change in society is often accompanied by personal and/or professional torment. Two examples of controversies from the early days of fire management come to mind. (Biswell's account of these controversies can be found on pp. 100–108.) The first was associated with a public hearing and post-fire analysis following a human-caused wildfire near Hoberg's Resort in Lake County in the early 1960s. This was the area where Doc (his name to most of us students) had done some of his early prescribed burning, with Mr. Hoberg's blessing. The wildfire came up to the edge of the resort as a crowning fire and dropped to the ground at the edge of Doc's burn unit, where it was controlled. I found the transcripts of the hearing while browsing through the unindexed stacks of the UC Berkeley Forestry Library. At the hearing, Biswell noted that, in his opinion, the fire had stopped because the fuels had been reduced in the prescribed burn area over several short-interval burns. Yet the agency people involved testified that the wind stopped exactly at the edge of the prescribed burn unit, so therefore a change in weather was responsible for the change in fire behavior. They were probably right that the wind slowed, but it slowed because the prescribed burned area had a dampening effect on the wildfire's behavior. I was able to visit the site years later, and I found all the trees dead in the wildfire area and a healthy forest in the prescribed burn area, proving what should have been obvious soon after the wildfire.

At roughly the same time as the hearing, UC Berkeley issued a press release on Harold's research, in which he was quoted as saying the kinds of things he was to repeat for the next three decades: that the early forests of the Sierra Nevada were sustainable because of fire, not in spite of it; that the interaction between forest and flame was a product of nature; and that sustainable forest management demanded a return of prescribed fire. Those of us who knew Biswell had all heard one or more variation on this theme, but a response to the press release from a statewide fire prevention organization called his statements "opinionated misinformation being spread by some people with quotable positions." To them, a person was either totally against the use of fire or ignorant.

Harold was an advocate of fire prevention, but he believed that there was a critical balance between fire suppression, prevention, and use. Smokey the Bear just couldn't say it all in one sentence anymore. A continual barrage of attacks and accusations followed Harold Biswell around the state during this period of the late 1950s and early 1960s. One had to be very courageous in those days, and it's easy for us to forget those times. A lesser man might have retreated, but Harold strode on, focusing on spreading his message and taking the high road in terms of his professional demeanor. The logic of that message led many of us, including me, to become interested in fire science as a career.

The burning at Hoberg's Resort in was one of the first successful wildland-urban interface fire projects, and in the book Biswell presents evidence of both his innovative outlook and his practical approach. Later, as he focused on mixed-conifer forests, he and his colleagues and students investigated soils, hydrology, fuels, and air-quality effects of fire. His innovative ideas remained controversial during the late 1960s, but his tireless public education efforts attracted a growing crowd of converts, including the National Parks Advisory Board. Biswell began to hold occasional prescribed burning tours, which soon grew in frequency and attendance. This period was a turning point in the profession's views on fire, but making that transition wasn't easy. Few of us will ever experience the professional hurdles faced by Harold and his contemporaries.

Where have we come since 1989, when this book was first published? We have made great strides in some areas, and we seem to be mired in the muck in others. The technology to conduct prescribed burns continues to improve. We now have computer models that successfully combine fire behavior information with geographic information systems to predict fire spread across landscapes. We have more sophisticated fire effects models to predict the ecological outcome of fire. We can tell which size classes of various tree species on a site are likely to die in fires with various flame lengths. Our technological fixes are not complete, but in comparison to other for-

est disturbances, such as wind, insects, and disease, fire technology is at the head of the pack.

However, do we use this technology effectively? Biswell's
Chapter 7 explains why we didn't use the technology of the
1980s to do more prescribed burning, and the case remains
strong that we could do much more. The phrase "forest
health" emerged in the late 1980s to explain why we see so
many trees dead and dying across the western landscape
(high-density, multilayered forests caused by fire exclusion are
at the root of the problem). Insects and disease epidemics are
at historic heights, and intense wildfires are expanding like
never before in the West. We continue to despair at the state
of our forests, but the solutions have become mired in political
debates. Elsewhere there are some radiant examples of fire
use: California state parks are burning in a wide variety of forest and shrub vegetation types; nature organizations such as
The Nature Conservancy have been using prescribed fire in
prairie restoration and oak woodland maintenance; and the
National Park Service is continuing to move forward with prescribed fire plans in chaparral and forested portions of national park system lands. These programs are complex. They
require understanding how plants and animals respond to fire
and how fire interacts with other ecosystem processes. They
also offer information on the effects of varying the season of
burning, as well as what happens when there are changes in
the frequency, intensity, or extent of the fire. The people who
started and built these programs almost always refer to one of
Harold Biswell's fire ecology workshops as the starting point
for their program.

The national forests will see expanded fire programs in the
coming years, too. Biswell's idea in the 1950s of using the
large federal emergency firefighting fund up front to do fuel
treatment was recently championed by Secretary of the Interior Bruce Babbitt on behalf of all the federal land management agencies. It made perfect sense forty years ago, but it
took almost half a century to become part of the fire culture. A
portion of the fund became authorized and available in 1998
for prescribed burning on all federal lands. This will have a

tremendous impact on project funding and will result in much more prescribed fire, and reduced threat of wildfire, over millions of acres of the West.

The intrusion of residences into wildlands, with the attendant fire problems, was always a major concern of Biswell's. In this book he warns of impeding catastrophic fire in the Berkeley Hills. His warning had precedence, not just prescience: one of the most devastating urban-wildland interface fires prior to 1991 occurred in the Berkeley Hills in 1923. A fire started in the hilltop area, and blown by hot, dry autumn winds, it swept down right to the edge of the University of California campus. Fire marshals were considering dynamiting entire residential blocks to save the rest of the town when fog blew in from the Golden Gate and helped to extinguish the fire. The burned area sprouted back with residences, just as the brush and eucalyptus trees sprouted back, and the residences spread farther into the wildlands over subsequent decades. The Berkeley Hills are not unique in this regard; they are but one of innumerable communities where residences are invading wildlands. But Harold lived in the Berkeley Hills, so it was of special interest and concern to him. His late 1980s prediction of a major catastrophic fire there, potentially worse than the 1923 Berkeley fire, came true in 1991. No one was saddened more than Harold Biswell when the 1991 fire killed 25 people, destroyed over 3,000 homes, and cost more than $1.5 billion: it was preventable.

This growing fire problem in what is called the urban-wildland interface will continue to plague fire managers. Of all the institutional problems with fire, this is the most complex because it involves mostly private land; myriad jurisdictional problems for zoning, building codes, and fire protection; and continuing attitudes that the disaster will strike somewhere else, or that it will never strike twice. Biswell's message is as relevant today as it was a decade ago.

In wildlands, history does repeat itself. Fire environments of yesterday are those of today, and they will be those of tomorrow. California and the West are fire environments without parallel in North America. Harold Biswell would say that our mountains will always stand majestically, and dry summers and windy spells will always be part of our western heritage. We can only intervene in the fire behavior triangle by managing the vegetation. Biswell, through his many demonstration workshops and in this book, gave us the tools to manage change through controlled fire. It is now up to us to take up the torch.

James K. Agee
College of Forest Resources, University of Washington
November 1998

Foreword to the Original Edition

Fire was the first natural force and source of energy to be tamed by human beings. Heating and food preparation were two early uses of fire. Pretechnological food gatherers, hunters, and herders also employed fire to manage plant and animal life. In modern land-use practice, however, fire has been regarded until very recently as an entirely destructive force to be suppressed by all means and at all times.

Harold Biswell was among those few far-sighted ecologists who realized very early in his professional career that well-regulated fire can play a beneficial role today as it did in earlier times. After overcoming much prejudice and fierce opposition, he was the first in California to show, almost single-handedly, how fire can be turned through prescribed burning from a cruel master into a good servant. This book provides us with the testimony of his accomplishments over 40 years of thorough and persistent study, experimentation and observation, teaching, training, and demonstration of prescribed burning and vegetation management in California wildlands. It differs from other works on fire ecology and management by the unique, personal message it conveys—that is, it blends scientific ecological knowledge with the wisdom and expertise derived from long practical experience and true insight.

He has laid the foundations for an overall reappraisal of the role of fire in the California wildlands, not only in such areas as wildlife conservation but also for forestry, livestock production, nature conservation, and natural resources in general. This work culminated in the development of the science and art of prescribed burning, which is described in this book in a clear, concise, and straightforward way with numerous, well-illustrated examples. Biswell presents his material not as isolated scientific and ecological techniques, but as imbedded within a broad range of interrelated physical, biological, ecological, socioeconomic, and cultural contexts. His basic philosophy and guideline is to work in harmony with nature and not to violate it, as, by contrast, do the futile attempts to virtually exclude fire. In this way, without specifically mentioning it, he applies the holistic landscape ecology approach that so strongly recognizes the need to create a viable symbiosis between the natural and human elements in wildlands.

Biswell's arguments derive strength from his long, active, and intimate involvement with all phases and scales of prescribed burning, enabling him to persuade his students (some of whom later became leaders in this field), as well as many professional land managers, users, and decision makers, of the value of the approach.

I studied under Biswell as a visiting research scientist from Israel in the late fifties, when he was called "Doc" by his students and admirers and frequently introduced as "Harry the Torch" or "Dr. Burnwell." Like my colleague, Dr. Liacos from Greece, I was highly impressed by his work, and we realized that the principles derived from it have far-reaching implications for the Mediterranean region, with its similar dry-summer fire climate and comparable vegetation types. Since then we have zealously spread the message of the benefits to be derived from controlled fire and fuel management in the Mediterranean Basin. In this region, the prejudices and misconceptions about the function of fire, and the constraints on initiating innovative research on the use of fire in enlightened management of wildlands vegetation, are even stronger than they were in California. In contrast to the instructive example of control burning by Indians in California, as well as by aborigines in Australia, fire has been—and still is—abused by Mediterranean pastoralists. This destructive practice, along with uncontrolled grazing, has caused the important role of fire as a selective force in the evolution of Mediterranean vegetation and in the maintenance of its productivity and diversity to be completely overlooked. Judged, like goat grazing, from its ill effects when abused, fire is regarded as wholly condemnable at all times and in all instances, and its controlled use as an effective means for fuel reduction is rejected. Even its use for research and experimentation is prohibited in many Mediterranean countries. Not only foresters but also most conservationists are fiercely opposed to prescribed burning in nature reserves and parks because they believe that it may endanger a much cherished, but illusory, sclerophyll forest climax (that is, the final stage of ecological succession in broad-leaf forests). However, the threats from destructive wildfires in dense and highly flammable pine and oak forests and shrub thickets are not less severe than in California. At the same time, the communication gap between academic researchers and public and private land managers is even greater than in California: the researchers either do not know about the pressing problems of the land managers or do not bother to present their results in a comprehensible and applicable way; and the land managers are not aware of, or are not willing to make use of, relevant new research information and management techniques. For these reasons, this unique book, although written from a California perspective, should be of great value to a broad international audience, but especially to Mediterranean peoples.

I am convinced that this book will serve as a vital source of information and inspiration for all—in California and elsewhere—who care about the fate of their wildlands.

Zev Naveh
Professor of Landscape Ecology
Technion-Israel Institute of Technology
Haifa

Acknowledgments

After walking through the Calaveras Big Trees State Park in 1977 and seeing our work there on prescribed burning, Ernest Callenbach, of the University of California Press, suggested to me that a book on this subject should prove interesting and worthwhile for many people. Within two weeks a contract for a book was signed.

When Elgy Kryger, watershed field supervisor of the Office of Fire Service Coordinator in San Diego, learned about the contract, he insisted that the book be for the general public, not just for fire scientists. He recommended that it be short, straightforward, readable, and well illustrated with photographs. These features pretty well describe this work.

I want to thank my wife for her never-ending help in writing this book. I am also grateful to several of my students who studied fire ecology and prescribed burning and inspired me to continue working with fire in California wildland resources management: namely, James Agee, Jan van Wagtendonk, Ronald Wakimoto, Lin Cotton, Robert Gartner, Carol Rice, Leonidas Liacos and Vasilious Papanastasis of Greece, and Zev Naveh of Israel. Special thanks are due James Agee for reading a large part of the manuscript and making valuable suggestions. Others who warrant thanks are Glenn Walfoort, California State Parks, for his fine help and expertise in prescribed burning in ponderosa pine, mixed-conifer, and giant sequoia forests, and for his intelligent understanding of prescribed burning; John McMillan, U.S. Forest Service, who gained field experiences by working with us at the Calaveras Big Trees State Park and who is doing prescribed burning in pine plantations; Marvin Dodge, California Department of Forestry, for helping with my teaching of university extension courses; Walter Graves, farm advisor, San Diego, for his testing of various grasses on freshly burned-over poor chaparral soils in southern California and for his championship of science above politics in resource management decisions; and to Gary Reece, program manager of the Watershed Fire Management Program in San Diego, for his help and expertise in handling prescribed fires. I am also grateful to Wayne Schultz, former owner and manager of Berkeley Photo, for his help in selecting photographs that would reproduce well; and to Paul Bishop, Jr., for his excellent work in developing the photographs.

Lastly, I thank the California Department of Parks and Recreation for employing me for eight years as special consultant to initiate its prescribed-burning program and to teach its rangers and ecologists the science and art of prescribed burning. This position made it possible for me to prescribe burn in many different vegetation types.

Introduction

This book describes the ecology and the use of fire in wildlands vegetation management. It emphasizes (1) the role of natural fires set by lightning in prehistoric times and the importance of understanding and working in harmony with nature, (2) the environmental impacts of excluding fires from wildland environments, and (3) the why, where, when, and how of prescribed burning (also known as controlled, or control, burning) to protect and enhance the wildland resources.

In this introduction I present the rationale for prescribed burning and describe how my background led me to heed and espouse that rationale. In Chapter 1 I examine the fundamentals of fire behavior and the factors that determine how fires burn. Chapter 2 is a discussion of the natural role of fire in ecosystems before the days of European settlement—that is, fires set by lightning and by the Indians. The histories of wildfires, on the one hand, and of prescribed burning, on the other, are then presented in Chapters 3 and 4. In Chapter 5 I discuss prescriptions and techniques of prescribed burning and how to put together a fire management plan. As will be seen, burning affects many different resources, all of which are discussed in Chapter 6. The concluding chapter presents the reasons (or excuses) given for not doing more prescribed burning.

An evolving philosophy about prescribed burning begins by reflecting on fires set both by lightning and by Indians during primeval times, fires that spread freely over the landscapes and served to recycle fuels and renew the vegetation. (See Figures

1

Figure 1. *"The friendly flame" in the understory of ponderosa pine. The prescribed fire (also called a control burn or a broadcast burn) reduces the fuels and structures the forest to make it largely fire-resistant. The fire is moving ½ to ¾ foot per minute. The area will need a reburn in five to seven years.*

Figure 2. *A prescribed fire in southern oak woodland-savanna.*

1–3.) It was only about 100 years ago that people decided that all wildland fires were harmful and determined to suppress them as quickly as possible. This practice has allowed unnatural changes to take place in the vegetation and caused fuels to build up, making some present-day wildfires so intense that they cannot be stopped until the weather changes or they approach natural fuel breaks such as bodies of water or recently burned areas. (See Figures 4–5.) Fierce wildfires burning in large volumes of highly flammable fuels during hot, dry summer weather under windy conditions are now doing tremendous damage to property and wildland resources and are hor-

Figure 3. *A reasonable facsimile of a primitive, open, parklike mixed-conifer forest. The ponderosa and sugar pine trees show hardly any effects of recurring surface fires, while the incense-cedar with its scaly fibrous bark shows the ease with which this tree can be blackened. Some ecologists describe this forest as a fire climax, meaning that it is maintained by recurring surface fires. Others describe it as a fire subclimax, meaning that if fire is excluded, the forest develops into a different type. This picture was taken two years after a prescribed fire in Yosemite National Park.*

Figure 4. *A once-pristine, fire-climax ponderosa pine forest until fire protection without any control burns enabled white fir to invade the understory.
Some people believe this invasion represents natural succession and are satisfied with what they see. But certainly it is not natural. How could it be when
ground-surface lightning-caused fires, one of the principal features of nature,
have been suppressed? The picture was taken in the Tahoe National Forest a
few yards south of the Placer County Grove of giant sequoias.*

ribly expensive to control. And that is not all! Each year the
wildfire situation worsens as suppression efforts become more
sophisticated. Inevitably, some of the wildfires of the future
will be more destructive of wildland resources and more dangerous to public safety and welfare than any fires of the past.

In view of this bleak situation, I have strongly recommended
that prescribed fires, carefully planned and set under the
proper conditions, be used in wildlands vegetation management. Such fires can mitigate the bad effects that would otherwise result from practices leading to intense wildfires. If natural fires set by lightning were once essential to the development
and survival of many types of vegetation, and the vegetation is

Figure 5. *A forest structure in ponderosa pine, created by prescribed burning. This structure illustrates how the forest reproduced naturally during primeval times in the presence of frequently recurring surface fires set by lightning. Reproduction is kept out of the understory while it thrives in the opening on the right, where there is barely enough surface fuel to carry fire beneath saplings (see far right background).*

still desirable to maintain, why don't we, then, purposely simulate them by setting fires on our own terms through prescribed burning? Such fires would be carefully set in selected places, at selected times, and under selected conditions of fuel moisture content, air temperature, relative humidity, wind direction and velocity, atmospheric stability, and weather predictions. And with the use of proven techniques, the flames would be managed and controlled. Thus, by prescribed burning and by working in harmony with nature, we could reduce debris and modify plant communities to make the vegetation more resistant to wildfires, thereby also helping to prevent damage and to reduce the costs of fire suppression. (See Figures 6–7.)

Figure 6. *Extreme accumulation of fuel in a mixed-conifer forest. Fuels of this type ensure that wildfires will be extremely intense, destructive, and difficult to control. Prescribed burning is an effective means of correcting this dangerous and unhealthy condition.*

Prescribed fires relate to nearly every aspect of the environment: the people, including their philosophies, politics, and laws; individual plants and plant communities; soils; wildlife; water and watersheds; diseases and insects; the atmosphere; and aesthetics. Combinations of interrelationships are nearly endless. And, of course, there are economic and sociological aspects related to every wildland management practice.

This book is intended to be useful to all segments of society and particularly to environmentalists and to resource practitioners involved in park and wilderness preservation, timber management, wildlife habitat improvement, range livestock grazing, watershed management, and recreation. To comprehend and fully appreciate prescribed burning, one must know that prior to European settlements, for thousands of years re-

Figure 7. *Prescribed burning in April in southern California oak woodland-savanna to reduce fire hazards and return the area to a more natural stable condition. Fire is backing down the slope at a measured rate of ⅝ foot per minute.*

curring lightning fires were a *natural* feature of the environment. Those fires were not ruinous. They maintained balance in ecosystems and ensured that the forests and other plant communities would reproduce, grow, and mature in good health and with vigor. How could this be, when no one tried to put out the fires? This question has been in the minds of many people in recent years as they read about and see on television the destructive wildfires that burn over thousands of acres of prime watershed lands, destroy precious timber, consume houses, and endanger the welfare and safety of countless people.

Wildlands fire management has three aspects: prevention, suppression, and use. They are equally important. Yet, over the years, great attention and support have been given to prevention and suppression, and rightly so, but very little to use.

Figures 8 and 9. *Before* (above) *and after* (below) *prescribed burning in ponderosa pine. Fuels on the forest floor have been reduced 57 percent, and the fire hazard is now very low.*

This is wrong. For if equal attention and support were to be given to all three aspects, fire suppression would gradually become easier and more effective, and the total costs of fire management activities would diminish.

In no way does this book advocate the lessening of efforts in wildlands fire prevention and suppression; these activities are essential. Instead, it advocates prescribed burning in wildlands vegetation management, since these fires can be highly beneficial in preserving and enhancing the vegetation and other wildland resources, as well as in reducing the wildfire hazards. (See Figures 8–9.)

This book is confined mostly to California's vegetation and conditions because that state is where I have done most of my research and study and where the wildfire problems are greatest. However, the ideas and principles involved should have wide application in other areas of the world where the vegetation is abundant and becomes excessively dry at some season of the year.

Certain features of the California environment make the wildlands extremely susceptible to fire occurrence and spread. Mild, moist winters are favorable to abundant plant growth; rainless, or nearly rainless, summers dry out the vegetation and soils; daytime temperatures in summer are usually high, and the humidity may be exceptionally low; winds are often strong; and in places the topography is rugged and steep. Dead fuels accumulate rapidly in this environment because winters are too cold and summers too dry for much bacterial activity; consequently, decay of organic matter is slow. In addition to these natural features, the great influx of people into California and the building of houses in areas of high fire hazards greatly complicate the wildfire problem. (See Figures 10–11.)

The Author's Background

My research, observations, and reading have convinced me that fire is natural to wildland environments and must be used. Lightning fires have always burned over our hot and dry summertime landscapes and always will. It is up to the public to determine whether the wildland fires will be gentle and bene-

Figure 10. *A prescribed burn through an area of young ponderosa pine. The burn killed most of the incense-cedar invading the understory, reduced fire hazards, and produced a diverse forest pattern.*

ficial affairs or raging holocausts that devastate the vegetation, soils, watersheds, and wildlife, and sometimes spread so relentlessly that they kill people and destroy homes.

My early background gave me much experience in vegetation management. It was on a highly diversified farm in the Ozark foothills of Missouri that I grew up, in a family of five girls and five boys. We tended pastures and raised beef cattle, sheep, hogs, and brood mares. Two or three cows and a few chickens furnished dairy and poultry products. Field crops were corn, wheat, oats, and hay of alfalfa, red clover, and timothy. (Today, soy beans are an important crop there.) About half of the 346 acres was nearly level bottomland, and the other half, hills. As a rule, we cultivated the level grounds, and let our livestock graze the hilly portions. Two large creeks passed through the farm; one was sandy and good for swimming, and

Figure 11. *Houses located in highly flammable fuels. Such buildings are a wildfire management problem. They also add to the risk of prescribed burning in nearby areas. A large number of houses of this sort are located both immediately above and below Calaveras Big Trees State Park, where prescribed burning has been in progress. Bear clover draped with pine needles and small twigs, along with small incense-cedar and white fir "ladder fuels" in the understory of large trees, is one of our most flammable and dangerous fuel types. This area should be prescribe-burned and cleaned to reduce the fire hazard to a tolerable level.*

the other was muddy with clay and loam. In both, fishing was good. Where the creeks meandered through cornfields, muskrats were plentiful.

The forests were hardwood of oaks, hickories, black walnut, and other species typical of that area. They had the potential for high-priced logs, as well as affording homes for many raccoons, opossums, skunks, mink, red squirrels, groundhogs, cottontail rabbits, and bobwhite quail. Cardinals and other songbirds were abundant. At present, all these wildlife species, plus deer, coyote, and wild turkey, are plentiful, except for groundhogs, which seem to be fewer, perhaps because of coyote predation.

It was on the farm that I first developed a respect for the land. We saw the need for tender care of soils. Slopes had to be managed with utmost care or the soil would wash away. I learned about the requirements of wildlife and how the habitat for each species can be improved. Every year at woodcutting time we made brush piles and left them for the cottontail rabbits, which we later hunted in the winter snow. I also learned about the importance of den trees for raccoons, squirrels, and owls. Those trees were protected. Selective cutting of trees for stove wood was a means of improving the forest stand. I discovered the beneficial effects of thinning on crop production by hand-thinning many miles of rows of listed corn. Each spring we did some burning of dry weeds and trash around the cornfields to help control plant diseases and insect pests. In managing livestock, I saw that animal numbers must be kept in line with forage and hay production. A farm boy learns an endless number of things about the environment and conservation, including crop rotation and the costs and returns of different methods of operation. One of the most valuable things I learned was the importance of hard work.

In October 1984, I visited the farm, now managed by my brother, Frederic. It is in excellent condition, with no visible soil erosion, thanks to tall fescue grass and good management.

I left the farm to attend Central College in Fayette, Missouri, where I majored in zoology. From there I went to the University of Nebraska and did graduate work in botany and plant ecology, with Dr. J. E. Weaver as my major professor. He was an excellent teacher and example, but he rarely mentioned the ecology of fire. My M.S. degree was in botany and grassland ecology; my thesis concerned the effects of clipping on the yield of tops and roots of grasses in prairie sod. I received my Ph.D. in botany and forest ecology, with a minor in animal ecology, my dissertation dealing with the effects of the environment on the root development of deciduous forest trees.

My first employment was in range research with the U.S. Forest Service (USFS) at the California Forest and Range Experiment Station, now the Pacific Southwest Forest and Range

Experiment Station, in Berkeley. I worked one summer on mountain meadows and six years on mid-Sierran foothill woodland-savanna out of the San Joaquin Experimental Range in Madera County. In 1940, I was put in charge of range research at the Forest Service Southeastern Forest Experiment Station in Asheville, North Carolina. Part of my work was in the coastal plain of Georgia, where, in 1941, I was introduced to the use of low-intensity fires in the production of timber and forage in the piney woods.

After field surveys and a study of the literature and in response to people's interests and suggestions, I decided to experiment with rotational burning and livestock grazing in forests of longleaf and slash pines and wire grass. The primary objective was to maximize timber production; the secondary purpose was to improve grazing. These aims would be achieved by using fire to reduce logging slash, reduce brush in the understory of trees, prepare seedbeds, control brown spot disease on longleaf pine, and regulate fire occurrence and grazing to favor reproduction of longleaf and slash pines.

During the early forties, very little planned burning was done in the southeastern piney woods. However, there was a growing interest in this activity. Much confusion and controversy existed because the need for fire in forest management and for expertise in burning was little understood. Emphasis had been on fire prevention and suppression. Many foresters frowned on the use of fire, finding it difficult to understand the difference between a wildfire and a prescribed fire.

Early in the planning stage of the southeastern studies, I had an eye-opening experience. I was invited to see where foresters had been burning in the piney woods—an area of 80,000 acres of Brunswick Peninsula Company lands, now Union Camp. One elderly man had been assigned the job of burning. He worked alone, making full use of forest roads, past burns, and his experiences with fire behavior under varying conditions. Patient and skilled, he managed with full control of the flames. It was an important lesson: in using fire, both patience and experience are invaluable. My observations during this one day were sufficient to convince me that prescribed fires can be used beneficially in forestland management.

In 1947, I accepted a teaching and research position in the

Department of Forestry and Conservation at the University of California, Berkeley. Very soon I found myself involved in research on the use of fire in Sierran foothill woodland-savanna to improve ranges for livestock grazing and wildlife. I spent many weekends in the foothills working with ranchers in control burning to reduce and manipulate brush. During that period I also carried on a large project of burning chaparral in Lake County for game habitat improvement and sheep grazing. In the spring of 1951, I began studies on the use of fire in ponderosa pine in the Teaford Forest in Madera County near North Fork, and started a similar project in the fall of that year at Hoberg's Resort in Lake County. These studies continued through 1964. Some of the plots at Hoberg's are still in place, and I have examined them many times since their inception.

In 1961 and 1962, thanks to a Guggenheim award, I spent two months each summer in the Mediterranean region of Europe, studying the role of fire in various vegetation types there.

In 1965, I began studies of prescribed burning in giant sequoia and mixed conifers at Whitaker's Forest in Tulare County. This project was carried on until 1973, when I became professor emeritus at the university. For two years after formal retirement, I taught a course in fire ecology on the Davis campus of the university, and for eight years I taught university extension courses: forest fire ecology, chaparral fire ecology, giant sequoia fire ecology, and fire ecology basics. Popular and well attended, these were field courses requiring two full days (usually a Saturday and Sunday). When conditions were right, a demonstration burn added greatly to the quality of these sessions. The extension courses and field days together did much to promote better understanding of the important role of fire in wildlands vegetation management. Along the way I did some burning and instruction work in ponderosa pine forests in southern Colorado and in South Dakota.

From fall 1975 through 1982, I served as special consultant in fire ecology to the California Department of Parks and Recreation. In November 1975, prescribed burning was started in Calaveras Big Trees State Park, and spring 1978 in Cuyamaca Rancho State Park in San Diego County, as well as in Big Basin Redwoods State Park, a short distance south of San Francisco.

Since that time, prescribed burning has been used in several other state parks having different vegetation types and plant communities.

This background gives me confidence in suggesting that prescribed fires can be extremely useful in the management of wildland ecosystems. Since fire is related to nearly every aspect of the environment, there is no end to what one can learn about its fascinating role as a constructive, rather than as a destructive, force.

Vegetation

Listed here are the California plant communities, identified by key species and vegetation understories, in which I have used fires. (Scientific names are given in the index.)

Ponderosa pine forests   Ponderosa pine and California black oak, with an understory of shrubs such as manzanitas, bear clover, and grasses.

Mixed-conifer forests   Ponderosa pine, incense-cedar, sugar pine, white fir, Douglas-fir, and California black oak, with an understory of shrubs such as ceanothus and manzanita species, tanbark oak, dwarf tanbark, and chinquapin.

Giant sequoia forests   Giant sequoia, white fir, and sugar pine, with an understory of hazel bush, dogwood, ceanothous species, California wild rose, and lupines.

Redwood forests   Redwood, Douglas-fir, tanbark oak, and madrone, with an understory of California huckleberry, ferns, and wood-sorrel.

Knobcone pine forests   Knobcone pine, with an understory of manzanita and ceanothus species and perhaps chamise. (See Figure 12.)

Torrey pine forests   Torrey pine, with an understory of forbs and shrubs.

Monterey pine forests   Monterey pine, with an understory of briars, poison oak, and grasses.

Foothill woodland-savanna   Blue oak, interior live oak, and digger pine, with an understory of ceanothus and manzanita species and a ground cover of annual grasses and forbs.

Figure 12. *A typical knobcone pine forest. The mature trees are small, the bark is relatively thin, and understory debris is abundant. The natural ecology of this forest is for fire to burn the entire forest stand and regenerate a new crop of seedlings. Since the cones are tightly closed (serotinous) and shed their seeds only after fire, prescribed burning should be done only in late fall, not in spring; otherwise most of the seeds will be destroyed by rodents and birds during the summer and not enough of them will remain to regenerate the forest. This is probably the case with all pines that produce serotinous cones.*

Southern oak woodland-savanna   Coast live oak, California black oak, Coulter pine, and canyon oak, with an understory of manzanita, ceanothus, and herbaceous vegetation.

Climax chaparral   Chamise, scrub oak, ceanothus and manzanita species, and western mountain-mahogany, with hardly any ground cover beneath the shrubs.

Forest chaparral   Possibly manzanita or ceanothus, perhaps with bear clover in the understory.

Southern coastal sage scrub   California sagebrush, white sage, and Wild buckwheat, with annual grasses intermixed.

Northern coastal scrub   Coyote bush, monkey flower, California blackberry, and woody lupines, with grasses and forbs intermixed.

Coastal prairie   Creeping wild rye, California oat grass, and velvet grass, with several annual grasses and forbs intermixed.

Eucalyptus   Eucalyptus, with an understory of annual grasses.

As far as I can determine, all these plant communities are fire-dependent; that is, in each case the dominant species and the structure of the community manifest an adaptation to some condition of fire frequency and intensity. Plant communities are discussed further in Chapter 5 (see page 126).

Literature on Prescribed Burning

Because this book is based primarily on my own research and field experiences in prescribed burning, plus an analysis of the literature over many years, I have not documented the text (and deluged the reader) with reference after reference. Rather, I have listed a few supplemental readings at the end of the text.

For those who wish to delve further into the literature on fire and prescribed burning, I recommend several publications, including several readily accessible books (see suggested readings for the Introduction, page 235).

Chapter One

Fundamentals of Fire Behavior

Anyone planning prescribed burning should first learn the fundamentals of fire behavior: how fires burn as influenced by characteristics of the fuel, weather, and topography.

Those who have tended fireplaces already know quite a bit about fire behavior. Surprisingly, *nearly all the basic principles observed in the fireplace also apply in wildland ecosystems*—a good fact to keep in mind while reading this book. The fireplace fire is used to keep warm, but it also has another purpose—the enjoyment of watching the fire as well as smelling an occasional puff of smoke. It lifts the spirit and creates both a friendly and cheerful atmosphere for lively conversation and a comforting ambience for contemplation.

From fireplace experiences, one knows that the combustion process occurs in three stages: first, the smoke and moisture vapors from the fire warming the fuels; second, the flaming process; and third, the afterglow as the fuels finally burn out (and, of course, it's the radiant heat from this afterglow that toasts those marshmallows). One also knows from fireplace experiences that cured, dry wood burns more readily and gives off more heat than freshly cut wood. In fact, it is difficult to get green wood to burn at all. Split wood dries rapidly and will ignite and burn more quickly than large round logs. Wet wood and green leaves give off more smoke than dry wood. After the fire becomes hot, the smoke is blue and minimum in amount.

To get a fire started, fine fuels such as pine needles and small twigs are placed underneath the large fuels, and there the fire is set. These fine fuels are arranged to form a porous bed. If the fire does not start quickly, a little breeze from the bellows or a blow of breath will help. The fire may burn slowly at first, but as the fuel becomes heated, the flames become longer and the fire more intense. If a large amount of dry wood is placed on the fire, it might become too hot, in which case some green wood of high moisture content or a few sprinkles of water can be added to cool the fire down. Wood for the fireplace is kept in a shed or other dry place because rain or snow dampens it so it will hardly burn.

Fire Behavior Parameters

One way to evaluate fire behavior and fire potential is simply to apply knowledge gained from past experience with specific fuel and vegetative types under known environmental conditions. This is the approach that most of us learn by prescribed burning. A more technical approach is to evaluate fire behavior by rate of fire spread and growth, fire intensity, and flame length.

Rate of Fire Spread and Growth

The rate of fire spread has the dimension of velocity. The most common velocity measurement used in forestry is chains per hour, a surveyor's chain being 66 feet. Other units of measurement may also be used. I use feet per minute. The rate of fire spread is affected by wind, slope, fuel bed characteristics, and particle properties.

Growth in size of burned areas is usually expressed in terms of acres burned per hour or per day. And, like the rate of spread, it is also affected by characteristics of the fuels, wind, and slope.

Fire Intensity

Two measurements of fire intensity have been developed. One is *reaction intensity*: the rate of heat released in the combustion process per unit of area beneath the fuel bed. The other is *fire-line intensity*: the rate of energy released per unit of fire front per unit of time, such as British thermal units per foot per second (Btu/ft/s).

A British thermal unit is the amount of heat required to raise the temperature of one pound of water (one pint) by one degree Fahrenheit at a specified temperature. When wildland fuels are completely burned, the heat yield is about 8,000 Btu per pound, being slightly higher with some, such as eucalyptus fuels with their oils. Fire intensity may be expressed by the formula $I = HWR$, where I is fire intensity; H is the heat yield of combustible fuel, which, as we have noted, is about 8,000 Btu per pound; W is the weight of fuel consumed in pounds per square foot; and R is the rate of spread of fire at the flaming front in feet per second. (See Figures 13–14.)

The National Fire-Danger Rating System of the Forest Service

Figure 13. *Loose structure of fuels permitting rapid drying and plenty of oxygen, in Cuyamaca Rancho State Park in San Diego County. Such a structure is highly flammable. The fuels here are chiefly dead branches of Palmer's ceanothus and snowberry, which can be very dry and highly flammable in late fall when draped with pine needles. A low-intensity prescribed fire through this area would greatly reduce the dead materials and fire hazard.*

Figure 14. *Worrisome heavy brush and dead debris surrounding a Coulter pine in beautiful Heise County Park in the mountains east of San Diego.*

uses indexes to aid in planning wildfire control activities. One of these is the Burning Index (BI), from the use of free-burning fires as models to indicate the energy release per unit length of fireline and rate of spread components. Fireline intensity is thus related to flame length. Most control burning prescriptions include some measure of fireline intensity.

Flame Length

Since the average length of flames at the edge of a free-burning fire is related to the fireline intensity, a third way of evaluating fire behavior is by the average length of flames.

Factors That Affect Fire Behavior

The three basic environmental factors that govern fire behavior are fuel, weather, and topography. The best way to learn how these interact is through observing prescribed fires in many different vegetation types and under varying environmental conditions. There is no substitute for experience and close observation.

Fuel

Characteristics of fuels that influence the way fires burn are the moisture content of dead and living plants; the ratio of dead to living materials; the ratio of fine to coarse materials; loading (the quantity of flammable debris per unit of land area); the arrangement of materials (sometimes called fuel-bed porosity); the continuity of fuels—that is, their distribution over an area or over the landscape; and the presence and amount of ether extractives. Minerals do not burn and, indeed, some can inhibit combustion. (See Figures 15–17.)

Figure 15. *Typical action of a prescribed fire in eucalyptus fuels. The high oil content and loose structure of the debris cause the fuels to burn vigorously. The fuel-stick moisture content here is 18 percent, the temperature 56° F, and the humidity 43 percent. The fire is backing down the slope at a rate of ¾ foot per minute.*

Figure 16. *A prescribed fire in 100-hour time-lag fuels in the understory of second-growth redwood in Big Basin Redwood State Park. The fuel consists of limbs that were killed by shading as the redwood trees grew and the stand thickened. The fire is moving at ½ to ¾ foot per minute and is removing a large portion of the debris, thus effectively reducing the danger of a severe wildfire.*

Moisture Content. In dead fuels (i.e., dead plant materials), moisture content is controlled primarily by precipitation, relative humidity, and temperature. The National Fire-Danger Rating System assigns dead fuels into subclasses according to the speed, or time lag, with which they lose their moisture. Four time-lag classes have been identified for forest roundwood fuels based on their size and litter depth:

Time Lag	Diameter of Materials	Litter Depth
1 hour	up to ¼ inch	up to ¼ inch
10 hours	¼ to 1 inch	¼ to 1 inch
100 hours	1 to 3 inches	1 to 4 inches
1000 hours	3 to 8 inches	4 to 12 inches

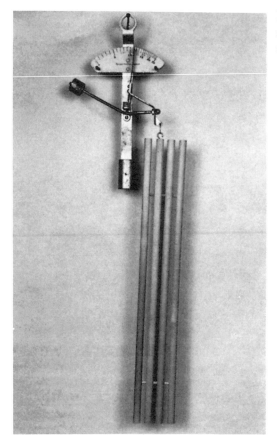

Figure 17. *Fuel-moisture sticks hanging from the scales used to weigh them.*

The moisture content of dead fuel can be measured with sufficient accuracy to serve as a guide in prescribed burning by weighing a frame of ½-inch ponderosa pine fuel sticks. The moisture content of the frame is equivalent to that of ten-hour time-lag fuels. This method is good because it tends to integrate the whole of the environment, including not only temperature and humidity, but the effects of varying day length and cloudiness.

The frame is a set of four ½-inch-diameter ponderosa pine dowels spaced ¼ inch apart on two hardwood pins. The overall frame is 2¾ inches wide and 20 inches long. It has an oven-dry weight of 100 grams. In the field, the frame is supported on a wire rack 10 inches above a bed of fine fuels such as pine needles, sawdust, or matted dry grass. For uniformity and comparison of data, the frame is placed in a north-south direction with the hook north, and is located so as to be in full sunlight at least from 9 A.M. to 5 P.M. After the frame has been placed in the field for a week or so and equilibrium between moisture content of the sticks and environment has been reached, the frame can be weighed with scales for that purpose. The amount in excess of the oven-dry weight of 100 grams is the percentage of fuel moisture. New frames should be used frequently because as they weather, they lose weight.

When burning in coniferous forests, woodland-savanna, chaparral, and grasslands, I have felt comfortable in setting fires when the dead-fuel moisture, as determined by fuel sticks, varies between 9 and 12 percent. For some of the more highly flammable fuels, such as that of coastal sage scrub and the debris of eucalyptus with their high content of ether extractives (resins and oils), the fuel moisture should be 12 to 15 percent for a low-intensity backing fire.

The live-fuel moisture—the moisture in the new growth of plants—affects fire behavior, particularly in chaparral, where the flames extend throughout the plant cover. This is the moisture content of twigs up to ¼ inch in diameter and in the attached leaves. As one might expect, live-fuel moisture is highest, perhaps 150 to 200 percent of dry weight, soon after new growth starts—that is, the weight of the moisture is one and a half to two times greater than the weight of the dry fuel. At this time, chaparral will scarcely burn at all, even if the dead fraction is 30 percent of the volume. Live-fuel moisture is generally down to 60 to 65 percent at the end of the long, dry summer period. It may stay near this low level throughout the fall if rains are at a minimum; however, with a few inches of rain in October, November, and December, it can rise by 10 to 15 percent. Prescribed burning is hazardous when the moisture is down to 60 percent. Occasionally, live-fuel moisture of 50 percent is reached during autumn Santa Ana winds. As the moisture rises above 75 percent, chaparral becomes harder and harder to burn.

Ratio of Dead to Live Fuels.   The larger the proportion of dead material, the more vigorously prescribed fires burn. For annual

Figures 18 and 19. Above: *Before a burn.* Below: *One year after the burn.*
Southern coastal sage scrub, in which the twigs are mainly less than ¼ inch in
diameter and high in ether extractives, is an extremely flammable fuel. An-
nual grasses are likely to increase as a result of burning, but this change does
not materially reduce the rate of fire spread. The hazard of this type of fire is
reduced by small frequent burns in spring or early summer.

grasses, the entire plant cover is dry by midsummer and is highly flammable. Coastal sage scrub is much the same way, partly because of the annual grasses that normally grow in the plant cover. (See Figures 18–19.) For chamise chaparral, the dead fraction for the first ten years after a fire is so small that the plant cover will scarcely burn. However, the dead fraction increases with the age of the chaparral. At 20 years of age, it will be about 20 percent; at 30 years, 30 percent; at 40 years, 40 percent; at 50 years, 45 to 50 percent. With the ratio of dead to live fuels gradually widening with age, one can expect a some-what similar increase in fire intensity. Wildfires in 50-year-old chaparral, burning under severe fire weather conditions, can be so intense that some become virtually unstoppable. For this reason I have suggested that chamise chaparral be burned in rotation every 30 years to keep the ratio of dead to live fuel at a level at which wildfires can be controlled. With this frequency, and surrounded with areas of more recent burns and less dead fuels, a prescribed fire can be easily managed and not too diffi-cult to handle. (See Figure 20.)

Ratio of Fine to Coarse Materials. The fine fuels—for example, the one-hour time-lag fuels—absorb heat and dry quickly. They will ignite and burn when the larger fuels are not yet dry enough to burn. This feature enables one to prescribe-burn in forested areas to reduce the fine fuels and the total fuel volume a little at a time. Examples of fine fuels in forested areas are pine needles, bear clover, grasses, and small twigs less than ¼ inch in diam-eter. In grasslands and coastal sage scrub, fine fuels make up most of the fuel volume; for chamise, it is about 65 percent.

Loading. Fuel volume, or loading, is expressed in pounds or tons per unit area. Volume usually refers to the total of all vege-tation in grasslands, coastal sage scrub, and chaparral, but in forests it may mean only the fuels subject to burning in a pre-scribed fire. The fuel load in grasslands may not be more than 2 or 3 tons per acre; in climax chaparral, it may be up to 45 tons, depending on the species and the productive capacity of the site. A thin, low-growing cover of chamise on poor soil may not weigh more than 10 to 12 tons per acre, but a dense chaparral

Figure 20. *Prescribed burning with a low-intensity fire in Torrey Pines State Reserve, near Del Mar, San Diego County. The fire will back downslope to the fireline created by raking debris from a hiking trail. The park ecologist will see that the fire does not cross this line. The person in the background is a visitor from a nearby home.*

cover of scrub oak on north-facing exposures of deep soil may weigh as much as 40 to 45 tons. This difference is important because intensity of fire tends to increase with the weight of the fuels burned. In protected forests, where large logs lie on the ground, the fuel load may be as high as 150 to 200 tons per acre, or even more.

Arrangement of Fuels.   Whether fuels are loosely arranged, as with coarse ponderosa pine needles, or closely arranged and compacted, as with smaller white fir needles, can make a big difference in fire behavior. The loose arrangement of coarse pine needles results in good ventilation and rapid drying of the needles and, in burning, permits plenty of oxygen to reach the fuel. By contrast, white fir needles form a dense mat that hardly permits any ventilation in the fuels or any available oxygen; so they burn poorly. Sugar pine needles are about one half as large as ponderosa pine needles and therefore form a fuel mat of intermediate compactness and flammability.

Continuity of Fuels. The uniformity of fire spread is particularly affected by the continuity of fuels. In forested areas, one of the most important considerations in prescribed burning is the fuel that carries the fire. What is it? That is always my first question concerning the potential for prescribed burning in an area I have not seen. A highly flammable fine-surface fuel, such as ponderosa pine needles, California black oak leaves, or dry grasses, over the area to be burned is usually desirable. If this surface fuel is broken here and there by other, less flammable types of fuels, a prescribed fire will need more watching to keep it burning uniformly. On the other hand, breaks in the continuity of fuels can lead to greater diversity of cover and in many cases facilitate fire handling.

Ether Extractives. Large amounts of ether extractives—components that can be dissolved by ether and removed from the plant material—in the fuel can measurably increase flammability. Examples are volatile oils in black, purple, and white sages, in eucalyptus, and in chamise; waxes in dry cheat grass and annual ryegrass; and resins in dead ponderosa pine needles and on sugar pine cones. These extractives increase in amount during the hot, dry summer months, and the plants become more flammable as the summer advances. Incense-cedar and bear clover are particularly vulnerable.

Weather

Aspects of weather to consider in prescribed burning are air temperature, relative humidity, and wind velocity and direction. All three of these are easily measured, but when they are interrelated with one another and with the fuels and topography, interpretation and prediction become difficult.

Air temperature determines to some extent how easily fires

ignite and how rapidly they spread. It directly affects ignition because the amount of heat required to raise the temperature of fuels to combustion, approximately 610° F, depends on their initial temperature. When the temperatures of air and fuels are high, it doesn't take much additional heat for ignition. Any little spark from friction or a piece of glass in the sun can start a fire—which helps explain why so many fires occur during the extremely hot days of summer. On the other hand, if the air and fuels are both cold, more heat must be applied to get a fire going. Air temperature also affects the way fires burn, through its influence on local winds, fuel moisture, and atmospheric stability. In summary, everything else being equal, the higher the temperature, the greater will be the ease of ignition, the rate of fire spread, and the intensity of heat produced.

High temperatures can be a problem in prescribed burning in two respects. In understory burning, they can contribute to excessive scorching of foliage, and in all types of fuels, spot fires can increase and become troublesome when temperatures reach 85° to 90° F. In prescribed burning in forested areas, the recommended air temperature is 65° or less, and in chaparral and grasslands, the maximum is 90°.

Temperatures beneath forest canopies are usually a little lower than those in openings because the fuels are shaded. Clouds and wood smoke also have a cooling effect on fuels. During autumn and spring falling night temperatures can have a pronounced effect in cooling fuels and slowing the combustion process.

Relative Humidity.   Dead fuels either absorb moisture or give it up, depending on the amount of moisture in the atmosphere. So relative humidity is an important consideration in prescribed burning. Warm air can hold a great deal of moisture, cool air much less. Relative humidity moves up or down as the temperature changes. It approximately doubles with each 20° F temperature increase and is halved by a reduction of 20° F. This information is useful in planning and conducting prescribed burns. For example, in forests and chaparral, good seasons for burning are autumn and spring on sunny, warm days, because in late afternoon the air cools and fuel moisture increases. In these seasons, conditions for burning might be nearly ideal from about 10 A.M. to 4 P.M., after which the combination of cooling air and rising fuel moisture reduces the tendency of fire to spread.

Wind. In prescribed burning, wind can be beneficial in several ways. It accelerates oxygen supply and preheating of the fuel, increasing fire intensity and thereby making possible the burning of fuels that otherwise might not burn under cool, moist conditions. In understory forest burning, a light wind dissipates heat, thereby preventing scorching of crowns, particularly on level ground where, without wind, scorching can be severe. Finally, a light wind after rain or morning dew is helpful in drying out fine fuels and bringing them into burning condition.

Although light winds can be beneficial and often essential in successful burning, wind can also cause erratic fire behavior, because its velocity, direction, and stability are difficult to predict with precision. Changes in wind velocity and direction are perhaps the principal causes of fire escapes in prescribed burning.

In measuring and reporting wind speed, the National Weather Service uses a standard height of 20 feet above the ground or vegetation. For practical reasons, I measure and record wind velocities taken about 5 feet above the ground. In forested areas particularly, the velocities are considerably less than those at 20 feet because the trees have a moderating effect.

Winds follow normal patterns to some extent; for example, in the Sierra Nevada foothills, they start blowing upslope in the morning about 9:30 A.M. as the air near the ground warms, and blow downslope during the night as the air cools. This downslope movement might continue until 9 A.M. the next morning, because warm air is lighter than cool air. There is also a fairly well defined season of occasional dry, strong northeasterly winds extending from about the first of September through December. A second period of strong, but less severe winds occurs in February and March. In southern California, these winds are known as Santa Anas and in northern California as northeasterlies. Their frequency and duration for a ten-year period in

TABLE 1.   Santa Ana Wind Frequency and Duration
by Month for the Angeles National Forest
over a 10-Year Period, 1951–60.

Month	Average Number of Santa Anas per Month	Average Duration in Days	Average Number of Days per Month
January	0.7	1.7	1.2
February	1.0	1.9	1.9
March	1.7	2.5	4.3
April	0.8	1.8	1.5
May	0.7	1.4	1.0
June	0.4	4.5	1.8
July	0.2	2.5	0.5
August	0.0	0.0	0.0
September	1.1	4.4	4.8
October	1.9	4.5	8.6
November	2.6	5.0	13.0
December	1.8	3.7	6.6

the Santa Monica Mountains of the Angeles National Forest are shown in Table 1. It is interesting that in this period no Santa Anas were recorded for August—the month when most of the lightning fires ignite in this area.

The dreaded Santa Ana winds arise when high-pressure systems develop over the intermountain states and low-pressure systems occur off the California coast. These strong descending winds must be avoided in prescribed burning. Careful attention must be given to charts showing the location of pressure systems and to the latest weather forecasts. When planning and setting prescribed fires, one should keep in mind the possibility that Santa Anas may develop at any time. Fires should be set so that they will be backing against a strong east or northeast wind in case a Santa Ana arises. Another precaution is to limit the acreage burned to the amount that can be completed in one day, so the fires can be extinguished quickly if necessary.

Topography

Fire behavior is related to topographic features of the landscape in several ways, some direct, others indirect. A fire burning on nearly level ground with little or no wind will rapidly increase in rate of spread when it goes uphill; and the steeper the slope, the faster that rate will be. For example, a fire burning on nearly level ground doubles in rate of spread when it goes up a 25 percent slope and doubles again when the slope is 40 percent. In moderate amounts of forest fuels, a prescribed fire backing slowly downslope at the rate of ½ to ¾ foot per minute, and with flames only 1 to 2 feet long, would go wild burning upslope, with flames perhaps 7 or 8 feet in length. This rapid step-up in fire spread occurs because the fuels ahead of the flaming front are dried and heated by convection and radiation. Local winds behind the fire also increase.

In moderate and heavy forest fuels, prescribed fires should be started at the tops of slopes, under proper fuel-moisture and weather conditions, and managed so they move downslope at the rate of ½ to ¾ foot per minute. We cannot modify slopes to reduce fire hazards, but we can fit the fires to slope conditions. In fact, slope can contribute to fire control and management. It is much safer to burn on slopes of 15 to 30 percent than on level ground. (See Figures 21–22.)

After fuels in forested areas have been reduced with two or three prescribed fires, it might then be desirable to prescribe-burn upslope to cover a large acreage in a short time.

Management of prescribed fires in chaparral is different from that in forested areas. Here, the fires are usually set under conditions in which they will not back gently downslope but will burn upslope as convection and radiation preheat and dry the fuels ahead of the flames. In this case, the fire will burn upslope rapidly with little lateral spread, making for a high degree of safety.

Slope can produce indirect effects on fire behavior. Fuels on south-facing slopes in full sunlight become drier and warmer than those on north-facing slopes, and the vegetation usually has features that make it highly flammable. In climax chaparral,

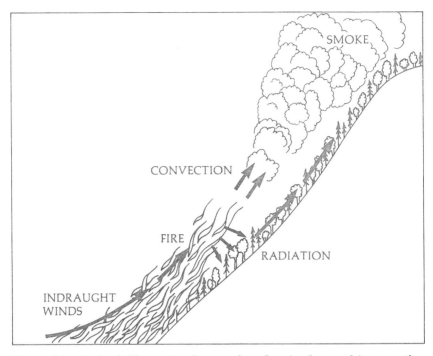

Figure 21. *A sketch illustrating how upslope fires in chaparral increase the rate of fire spread by drying and heating fuels ahead of the fire and by increasing wind velocity.*

for instance, one may find highly flammable chamise on the south-facing slopes and relatively less flammable chaparral whitethorn on north-facing slopes. In mixed-conifer forests, there may be highly flammable ponderosa pine needles on south-facing slopes and less flammable white fir debris on north-facing slopes. Such differences in flammability make it possible to burn on south-facing slopes when the north-facing slopes are too damp to burn. (See Figure 23.)

Elevation is also related to fire behavior because of differences in rainfall, temperature, and plant species. As rainfall usually increases with elevation, and air temperatures decrease, fuels are relatively less flammable at the higher elevations. So one might be able to prescribe-burn very well at the lower elevations while it is too cold and wet to burn at the higher ones.

Figure 22. *Upslope fire started with flame throwers in chamise chaparral in March while the surrounding grasses and flowers are still green. A wind of 5 to 10 mph in back of the fire will help it spread.*

Figure 23. *Pattern created by upslope burning in chamise chaparral. Burning with a breeze of 5 to 10 mph helps the fire spread under cool, moist conditions.*

Regulating Fire Behavior

Regulation of fire is based on the principle that the greater the amount of fuel consumed in a fire and the faster the fire spreads, the greater will be the fireline intensity and the flame lengths. This basic relationship ensures that the prescribed burner can regulate fire in two ways: by controlling the amount of fuel consumed in a single fire and by controlling the rate of fire spread.

The amount of fuel consumed in a prescribed fire can be governed by relating the time of burning to the fuel-moisture content. Experience and research have shown that fire behavior is very sensitive to changes in fuel moisture. Not only is moisture an excellent indicator of how a fire will burn, but it is easy to measure in the field. In principle, the higher the fuel moisture content, the smaller will be the amount of fuel consumed and the lower the intensity of the fire.

To obtain low-intensity fires in forest burning, the manager sets fires when the ten-hour time-lag of the fuel-moisture content is relatively high, perhaps in the 12 percent range. Exceptions to this rule do exist. In burning the deep duff of white fir and giant sequoia at Calaveras Big Trees State Park, we found that we could burn with smoldering fires, nearly flameless, when the fuel-moisture sticks gave a reading of 15 to 18 percent. In this case, a very high percentage of the fuels were consumed, but the fire moved only 3 to 5 inches per hour. There was practically no blackening of the tree trunks, and none of the foliage was scorched. The fires were first set in piles of heavy debris. As they burned, the fires dried the wet fuels just enough to keep the smoldering fires going.

To remove large amounts of fuel by using fires of moderate intensity, the burning is done when the fuel moisture is in the range of 7 to 8 percent. When it is below 7 percent, the amount of fuel is probably more important than the fuel-moisture content in affecting fire intensity. In chaparral, good fire control is achieved by burning uphill under conditions that deter the fires from spreading laterally.

Moisture content and flammability of fuels change at different rates in different types of fuels. Fine fuels such as pine needles dry quickly, whereas coarse fuels such as logs dry slowly. Because of this difference in drying rate, the manager can set fires when the fine fuels will burn but the coarse fuels will scarcely ignite. In this way, he or she regulates the amount of fuels consumed and, of course, the intensity of the fire itself.

Fire intensity can be governed also by regulating the rate of spread, since slow-moving fires produce less intensity than fast-moving ones. Fires for low intensity are either set at the tops of ridges so they will back gently downslope or set so they will back against a gentle breeze.

In understory burning in forested areas, there is always the risk that a prescribed fire will be too intense or will escape. This hazard is greatly reduced after two or three burns, when the fuel volume has become low. One can then burn uphill under conditions that allow the fire to spread rapidly, for the flames will lie close to the ground and, with a breeze dissipating the heat, there will be very little scorching of foliage.

Chapter Two

Fires Set by Lightning and by Indians

Fires from lightning and those set by Indians, prior to European settlement, had pronounced structural impacts on the vegetation. The evidence of these impacts is clear from early-day descriptions and pictures of the vegetation and is reinforced by recent research contrasting the changes that occur in places where fires are allowed to burn, either naturally or under control, with the changes at sites where fires are excluded.

Although the majority of the early-day descriptions are of ponderosa pine forests, some of the pictures show conditions in other forest types, such as giant sequoia. The fires modified the forest structure and burned out the debris; the net result was low fire hazards and high resistance to crown fires.

Structurally, recurring natural fires create broad spacings of trees, encourage the development of large specimens, and produce a mosaic of many different even-aged groups of trees. After a fire, a group of trees spring up in an opening left by the death of a mature tree or group of trees. The first fire or two that pass through after the trees have died consume the debris and leave a good seedbed for new reproduction, relatively free of pathogens and allelopathic (poisonous) substances. Ordinarily, when the new seedlings are only one to two feet tall, they cannot withstand light fires, but in this case they are largely protected in forest openings either by the lack of dry pine needles, or by grass, which—whether green or dry or sparse—

takes the brunt of the fires and thus keeps them from killing all the tree seedlings.

A second structural impact of recurring fires in pine forests is the formation of corridors and colonnades. These are formed by surface fires burning and killing pine seedlings on the border of openings. Border pine trees will drop sufficient needles each year to carry surface fires into the openings a distance one half to two thirds the height of the surrounding trees. For example, if the border trees are 100 feet tall, the corridor will be 50 to 65 feet wide. Trees on the edges of these corridors grow fast and become large, giving the appearance of colonnades. They add greatly to the visual qualities of pine tree forests. (See Figure 24.)

A third structural effect of recurring surface fires is the sculp-

Figure 24. *A natural corridor between two age classes of ponderosa pine. The corridor was created by surface fires burning through pine needles on the edge of the larger trees.*

Figure 25. *A fire scar. Every centuries-old giant sequoia has a fire scar at its base, testifying that it has withstood many lightning-set fires. But this should be considered a part of its natural ecology. Such trees add "sculptural value" to the visual qualities of giant sequoia groves. Views of the tree and its surrounding masterful sugar pines are being lost as white fir crowds the understory.*

tured appearance of fire scars at the base of trees. These are most pronounced on giant sequoias. A survey of many giant sequoias in several groves showed that every tree over 10 feet in diameter at breast height had a fire scar or other evidence of fire at its base. (See Figure 25.)

Forest openings such as those just described are ideal for excellent growth of new pine reproduction. They are large enough to provide overhead sunlight but small enough to allow side shading. This combination—good seedbeds, overhead lighting, and side shading—provides optimum growing conditions for new reproduction. Furthermore, the openings may be instrumental in trapping blowing snow, which provides favorable moisture to the new seedlings. The surrounding trees also ensure that there will be adequate seed for reproduction.

After pine trees in openings are 12 to 15 feet tall, they drop enough needles to carry surface fires. The first fire thins by killing some of the smaller trees, but the larger ones survive to form an even-aged stand. In some cases this might not be more than three to five specimens, but usually there will be more. Often the seedlings will come in thick.

In pristine forests, new seedlings continually sprang up under the older trees, but as fast as they appeared, they were killed by the next surface fire. In this way, forests were kept open and parklike and relatively free of understory competition. In pine forests, recurring fires continually acted as a thinning agent. In the young and pole-sized stands, such fires killed the suppressed trees—that is, the smaller, less vigorous ones—because of their thinner, drier bark. Nearly always, it is the suppressed trees that are killed by surface fires. In this way, the fires tend to select and favor the development of fast-growing, healthy trees, which is why they were important in the evolutionary development of the species.

With each surface fire in the older stands, a few fire-scarred trees are damaged enough in the new burn to topple over. In experimental work, I have found that fire-scarred trees surrounded with pine needles catch fire easily, but only about 1 percent of these burn enough to topple over sometime during the postfire year. When a tree is killed, the roots of the surrounding trees quickly appropriate the soil made vacant, and the trees show stimulated growth. In pristine forests, some of the trees became very large indeed.

The character and general appearance of pristine pine forests impressed early-day travelers and explorers, who described them in glowing terms. For example, in 1871 Clarence King, a geologist in Brewer's Geological Survey party, wrote:

Passing from the glare of the open country into the dusky forest, one seems to enter a door, and ride into a vast covered hall. The whole sensation is one of being roofed and enclosed. You are never tired of gazing down long vistas, where in stately groups, stand tall shafts of pine. Columns they are, each with its own characteristic tinting and finish, yet all standing together with the air of relationship and harmony. . . . Here and there are wide open spaces around which the trees group themselves in majestic ranks. . . .

Whenever the ground opened level before us, we gave our horses the reins, and went at a free gallop through the forest; the animals realized that they were going home and pressed forward with the greatest spirit. A good-sized log across our route seemed to be an object of amusement to Kaweah, who seized the bits in his teeth and, dancing up, crouched, and cleared it with the impression that one was enough of that sort of thing.

And here is John Muir, in 1894, describing the Sierra Nevada forests:

The inviting openness of the Sierra woods is one of their most distinguishing characteristics. The trees of all the species stand more or less apart in groves, or in small irregular groups, enabling one to find a way nearly everywhere, along sunny colonnades and through openings that have a smooth parklike surface, strewn with brown needles and burrs. . . . One would experience but little difficulty in riding on horseback through the successive belts all the way up to the storm-beaten fringes of the icy peaks.

C. E. Dutton gives an excellent description of the ponderosa pine forests of Arizona as they appeared in the Grand Canyon District, 1880–81:

The trees are large and noble in aspect and stand widely apart, except in the highest part of the plateau where the spruces predominate. Instead of dense thickets where we are shut in by impenetrable foliage, we can look far beyond and see the tree trunks vanishing away like an infinite colonnade. The ground is unobstructed and inviting. There is a constant succession of parks and glades—dreamy avenues of grass and flowers winding between sylvan walls, or spreading out in broad open meadows. From June until September there is a display of wildflowers which is quite beyond description. The valley sides and platforms above are resplendent with dense masses of scarlet, white, purple, and yellow. It is noteworthy that while the trees exhibit but few species, the humbler plants present a very great number, both of the species and [of the] genera. In the upper regions of the high plateaus, Mr. Lester F. Ward collected in a single season more than 600 species of plants, and the Kaibab, though offering a much smaller range of altitude and climate, would doubtless yield as rich a flora in proportion to the diversity of its conditions.

At a distance of about eight miles from its mouth, the ravine we have chosen has become very shallow, with gently sloping sides. At length we leave it and ascend its right bank to the upper platform. The way here is as pleasing as before, for it is beneath the pines standing at intervals varying from 50 to 100 feet, and upon a soil that is smooth, firm, and free from undergrowth. All is open, and we may look far into the depths of the forest on either hand.

S. B. Show and E. I. Kotok, two influential foresters who worked in California for many years, wrote in 1924:

The virgin forest is uneven-aged, or at best even-aged by small groups, and is patchy and broken; hence it is fairly immune from extensive crown fires. Extensive crown fires, though common in the forests of the western pine region, are almost unknown in the California pine region. Local crown fires may extend over a few hundred acres, but the stands in general are so uneven-aged and broken and have such a varied cover type that a continuous crown fire is practically impossible. A rare exception was the Egg Lake fire on the Modoc National Forest, where one area of 92 acres was destroyed. In general such stands are immune, but immunity to crown fires does not extend to second-growth stands, cut-over areas, or restocking brush fields.

In the Leopold Committee report *Wildlife Management in the National Parks*, addressed to Secretary of the Interior Stewart Udall in 1963, is this description:

When the forty-niners poured over the Sierra Nevada into California, those that kept diaries spoke almost to a man of the wide-spaced columns of mature trees that grew on the lower western slope in gigantic magnificence. The ground was a grass parkland, in springtime carpeted with wildflowers. Deer and bear were abundant. Today much of the west slope is a dog-hair thicket of young pines, white fir, incense-cedar, and mature brush—a direct function of overprotection from natural ground fires. Within the four national parks—Lassen, Yosemite, Sequoia, and Kings Canyon—the thickets are even more impenetrable than elsewhere [see Figures 26–27]. Not only is the accumulation of fuel dangerous to the giant sequoias and other mature trees, but the animal life is meager, wildflowers are sparse, and to some at least the vegetative tangle is depressing, not uplifting. Is it

possible that the primitive open forests could be restored, at least on a local scale? And if so, how?

Lightning-Set Fires

Many scientists who have studied the occurrence of lightning fires assume their frequency now to be about the same as that prior to European settlement, the main difference being that most fires today are quickly suppressed. Lightning storms are a *natural* feature of the environment, and so are the fires they start. One must remember that any naturally functioning pine forest ecosystem in California includes the factor of fire. (See Figure 28.)

An excellent account of lightning fires in California's national forests was presented by E. V. Komarek in 1967 at a Tall Timbers fire ecology conference held at Hoberg's Resort in Lake County. He reported that the number of lightning fires on Forest Service lands in California varied from about 200 to 1,700 per year. They occur most often at the higher elevations, where summer thundershowers are common, and their number decreases at the lower elevations.

The frequency of lightning fires in the lower foothill grasslands and valleys in southern California has probably been underestimated. Today their occurrence is overshadowed by fires caused by people. Records show that in July, August, and September of 1958 there were 39 lightning fires in the foothill wood-

---

Figures 26 and 27. *The result of fire exclusion in the Placer County Big Tree Grove in Tahoe National Forest. Before periodic fires were suppressed, these were beautiful open, parklike ponderosa pine forests. In recent years, the forest character has been changing as incense-cedar (above) and white fir (below) have crowded into the understory of pines and California black oak. The wildfire danger is high; it is possible to lose the entire stand in one afternoon. The forest is in urgent need of prescribed fires. In both scenes, prescribed burning would be easy because of the highly flammable pine needles on the ground, which would make it possible to burn when conditions were cool and moist.*

Figure 28. *Fuels of ponderosa pine that accumulated following an insect in-festation. All size classes are represented and since the logs have rotted to some extent, they are highly flammable. Prescribed burns in such fuels should be set when the humidity is above 60 percent, temperature below 40° F, and fuel-stick moisture content 12 to 13 percent. The fire should be set to burn gently downslope on a single front.*

lands and grasslands of Fresno, Madera, Mariposa, and Tulare counties. Many lightning fires at low elevations occurred in early August 1977, when some 1,200 were set up and down the state. Sightings on Mt. Diablo revealed that some of these were set on the ground in tinder-dry grass. Some lightning fires have occurred during very hot weather. For example, during the last few days of August 1967 when air temperatures soared over

100° F, there were seven lightning fires in the Angeles National Forest and 11 in the San Bernardino National Forest.

In a study of the frequency of lightning fires in an area of about 5 million acres of forest and brushlands from Yosemite National Park north to the Feather River, it was found that the number of fires between 1948 and 1958 varied from 50 to 300 per year and averaged over 100; 200 or more lightning fires in a season seemed to come at intervals of five to ten years. Another study checked the number of lightning fires suppressed in portions of the Sierra Nevada. For this study, two areas in Yosemite National Park were selected, one at the Tuolumne Grove of giant sequoias, the other near the Mariposa Grove. In the Tuolumne area 39 lightning fires were suppressed from 1951 through 1959; in the Mariposa Grove, 36. Similar data were obtained for an area near Sloat, in the mountains east of Chico, and for one at Pinecrest. At Sloat, 24 lightning fires were suppressed, and at Pinecrest, 18. Lightning fires were recorded for all four areas in every year except 1954, when there were none in the Stanislaus National Forest, as indicated in Table 2.

Very possibly, the present frequency and number of lightning fires differ from those in pristine times. Today there are

TABLE 2. Number of Lightning Fires in
Four National Forests, 1951–59

Year	Plumas N.F.	Stanislaus N.F.	Sierra N.F.	Sequoia N.F.
1951	268	11	36	18
1952	164	61	114	86
1953	85	73	66	106
1954	14	—	15	14
1955	155	30	18	18
1956	186	85	109	125
1957	36	19	33	25
1958	101	54	120	124
1959	78	51	95	85

more dead trees and dry fuels and thus greater opportunity for
fires to get started, but most of the fires are quickly suppressed.
Under pristine conditions, the fires burned until they went out
on their own; some may have persisted nearly all summer and
burned thousands of acres.

Under present-day conditions, lightning fires in heavy fuels
are a particular worry to fire management officers, not only because of the large number that might be started in a short time
under dry storm conditions, as in August 1977, but also because some of the fires occur in inaccessible places and cannot
be reached quickly by fire-fighting crews.

Natural-fire management programs in Sequoia-Kings Canyon and Yosemite national parks permit lightning fires at high
elevations to burn themselves out. Such fires usually originate
on a ridgetop or west-facing slope in a red fir community in late
summer and fall and burn an average of 85 acres by moving
slowly downslope. Between 1968 and 1978, 325 lightning fires
burned a total of 27,743 acres. Sixty-seven percent burned less
than one-quarter acre and only 4 percent burned more than 296
acres, the largest consuming 327 acres.

Indian-Set Fires

That fires were set by Indians before Europeans arrived in California is borne out by the first-hand observations of various explorers and naturalists, among them Galen Clark, for many
years the guardian of Yosemite; Dr. L. H. Bunnell, a member of
the 1851 Yosemite discovery party; and Joaquin Miller, the Sierra
poet and forester. As Miller wrote in 1887:

In the spring . . . the old squaws began to look for the little dry spots
of headland or sunny valley, and as fast as dry spots appeared they
would be burned. In this way the fire was always the servant, never
the master. . . . By this means, the Indians always kept their forest
open, pure and fruitful, and conflagrations were unknown.

With this description in mind, I examined Yosemite Valley
one late February as the snow melted. As the dry spots appeared, it was easy to visualize how two or three squaws could
have burned over the whole valley floor within a few days and

Figure 29. *Results of Indian-type burning in Yosemite Valley. A low-intensity fire beneath large pines burned the pine needles but went out at the edge of the large trees where the fuels became less flammable.*

also how the fires could have been small, patchy, and of low intensity. (See Figure 29.)

Why did the Indians burn? Geographers and anthropologists have offered several reasons: to improve forage for deer and hunting conditions; enhance visibility; facilitate travel; catch grasshoppers, lizards, and snakes; improve seed production; and clear brush and undergrowth.

The Indians of California found little or no need for agriculture. Food was plentiful, consisting of acorns and other seeds, wildlife, and seafoods along the coast and fish in the rivers. Acorns were their principal plant food. Oak trees were abundant over nearly all of California, just as they are now except where removed for agricultural reasons. Large valley oaks grew in the interior valleys, blue oaks and interior live oaks in the

Sierra Nevada foothills, live oaks along the coast, and scrub oaks, dwarf interior live oaks, and leather oaks in chaparral. California black oaks grew in ponderosa pine forests, canyon live oaks in the mixed-conifer forests and along the coasts, and huckleberry oaks at elevations of 5,000 to 10,000 feet. (And that's just a partial list.) Oak tree preservation was perhaps one of the reasons for the Indians' use of fire. Not only do oaks show high resistance to surface fires, but their reproduction is favored by fire. The Indians probably knew this.

If one examines the many bedrock mortars along the edges of ponderosa pine and California black oak in the Sierra Nevada, it is easy to conclude that the Indians spent many days there in late summer and early fall grinding acorns that they had gathered from the forests and foothills. Bedrock mortars occur in the Sierra Nevada all the way from northern to southern California. Excellent examples may be seen in the Cuyamaca Rancho State Park in San Diego County, with its beautiful stands of California black oaks, canyon oaks, and coast live oaks. Scrub oak is abundant in the chaparral. Perhaps the most spectacular bedrock mortars are those beside Highway 88, a short distance north of Jackson (about 40 miles southeast of Sacramento), where 1,158 grinding holes can be found on one rock.

Indians burned not only to preserve the oaks and facilitate acorn gathering but to reduce fuels and fire hazards. Evidently they observed that fires in heavy debris can be intense and harmful to oaks. They also burned to make surroundings safer for themselves during the hot, dry summer periods.

Yet some people find it hard to understand why or how Indians used fire. For instance, in 1959 C. R. Clar wrote in his book *California Government and Forestry*:

It would be difficult to find a reason why the Indian should care one way or another if the forest burned. It is quite something else again to contend that the Indians used fire systematically to "improve" the forest. Improve it for what purpose? . . . Yet this fantastic idea has been and still is put forth time and time again.

Mr. Clar probably had timber production in mind. Of course, the Indians didn't burn to produce more merchantable timber, but they did have those oak trees and acorn crops, hunting, fire hazards, and self-preservation in mind.

Some skeptics have suggested that Indians actually burned very little because they lacked both the manpower and the technological skills to burn large tracts of vegetation in a systematic or purposeful manner. What these skeptics fail to realize is that fires in summer in California's dry vegetation could burn for weeks and for miles before being stopped, perhaps by a river, autumn storms, or a change in the flammability of the fuels.

Indians reportedly often made use of small fires, although how they did this is puzzling to some people. In fact, such fires can be set in early summer before the vegetation becomes uniformly dry, and again in fall when cooling conditions at night can cause fires to go out. Furthermore, low-intensity fires are usually not exceptionally difficult to manage and control. An account of the aborigines' intentional firing of the countryside near Albany, Western Australia, is to the point:

We met . . . natives engaged in burning the bush, which they do in sections every year. The dexterity with which they manage so proverbially a dangerous agent as fire is indeed astonishing. Those to whom this duty is especially entrusted, and who guide or stop the running flame, are armed with large green boughs with which, if it moves in a wrong direction, they beat it out. . . . I can conceive no finer subject for a picture than a party of the swarthy beings engaged in kindling, *moderating,* and *directing* the destructive element, which under their care seems almost to change its nature, acquiring, as it were, complete docility, instead of the ungovernable fury we are accustomed to ascribe to it.

One of the best publications on Indian burning is a 1973 book by Henry T. Lewis, *Pattern of Indian Burning in California: Ecology and Ethnohistory.* Lewis' approach to the subject of Indian burning was quite different from that of most other anthropologists because he examined not only why but how burning was done, based on fire behavior related to fuels, weather, and topography and on results from present-day experiences in using fire. From his research on the Indian burning of coniferous forest zones, chaparral, and woodland-savanna, he concluded that a significant form of environmental management produced a dynamic balance of natural forces.

An increasing number of ecologists and conservationists are worried about the devastation caused by modern practices of

manipulating the environment. Consequently, they are won-
dering more about how Indians managed the habitats in which
they lived and of which they were a part ecologically. As Fred
Fertig, in the *Sierra Club Bulletin* of August 1977, put it: "Before
today's sudden popular interest in ecology and before the science of ecology, before the waste and raping of so much of the
American land, disturbing or destroying so many vital ecological systems, before all this, there was the American Indian—
our first ecologist."

The same view is expressed by Theodora Kroeber and Robert
F. Heizer in the Sierra Club's *Almost Ancestors: The First Califor-
nians* (1968):

Ecologically, Indians were part of a natural order between whose
people and the animal and plant life there was a well-nigh perfect
symbiosis. California was a place of unravished forests, streams, valleys, hills, and meadows. The Indians' preservation of the land and
its products for the ten thousand or more years of their undisputed
occupancy was such that the white invaders wrested from them a gar-
den, not the wilderness it salved their consciences to call it. Separated
as we moderns are from our roots in the good earth, it is not surpris-
ing that we have forgotten those vital connections between ourselves
and nature so well understood by the Indians. Dependent on everything from processed foods to cut flowers, plastic dishes to alloyed
tools, it is nearly impossible for us to experience the dangerous implications of breaking into the ecology of life. We try to live by everything artificial, nothing natural, opposing actually our one-time union
with nature.

It was no wonder that former Secretary of Interior Stewart
Udall could begin his influential book on the conservation crisis, *The Quiet Crisis,* with a chapter on "The Land Wisdom of
the Indians." Concluding that chapter, he wrote:

It is ironical that today the conservation movement finds itself turning
back to the ancient Indian land ideas, to the Indian understanding
that we are not outside of nature, but of it. From this wisdom we can
learn how to conserve the best parts of our continent.

This is where prescribed fires, simulating the fires that burned
during Indian times, come into play.

Dating of Fires

In forested areas, tree trunks contain a partial record of past fires, at least as far back as the oldest trees. A fire of moderate intensity burning a log or other heavy debris beside a tree often kills the cambium (the thin sheath that lies beneath the outer bark and builds new tissues that bring about the growth of a tree's girth) on one side, leaving the other side unharmed. A new layer of wood then starts to grow around the scar, which in turn may be injured by another fire. By looking at the scars and counting growth rings, we can date fires even centuries after they occurred.

Scientists had an opportunity for large-scale dating of fires in primitive forests of California when they conducted a study, from 1915 to 1929, of dry rot in incense-cedar. It is probable, of course, that some of those fires were set by Indians. In this study, more than 1,300 trees of incense-cedar were cut in six localities extending from Sloat, in the Plumas National Forest, Plumas County, to the Sierra National Forest in Fresno County. At that time, it was thought that dry rot might be related to fire scars, but mill studies at a later date proved that was not so. All the felled incense-cedars were in mixed-conifer forests at elevations of 4,300 to 5,600 feet. The evidence showed that fires occurred throughout this region on an average of every eight years from 1685 to 1889 (See Figure 30). In fact, the records reveal there were fires in the forests nearly every year, but they were widespread throughout the region only every eight years, perhaps during dry years when lightning strikes were frequent. In other studies of fire-dating in ponderosa pine forests, it was found that fires in Oregon occurred with about the same frequency, and in Arizona it was every six to seven years.

A detailed study of fire scars on 74 acres in the Stanislaus National Forest in the Sierra Nevada showed 221 distinct fires between 1454 and 1912, or one about every two years. This frequency seems reasonable because pine trees drop enough needles to carry surface fires every year. In fact, I demonstrated that one can burn twice a year in a productive and full-stocked stand of ponderosa pine—first when the pine needle drop is about one half over, or about November 10 in the lower pon-

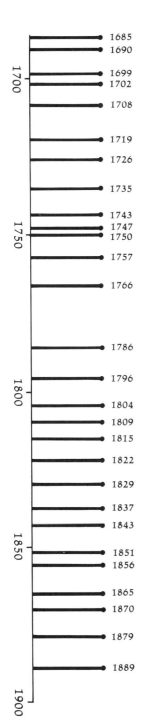

1685
1690
1699
1702
1708

1719

1726

1735

1743
1747
1750

1757

1766

1786

1796

1804
1809
1815

1822

1829

1837

1843

1851
1856

1865
1870

1879

1889

1700

1750

1800

1850

1900

Dates of Major Fires Throughout California
1685-1900

Figure 30. *Years during which fires in Califor-nia's Sierra Nevada forests were widely spread prior to organized fire protection. The fires at that time were set principally by lightning and were an important natural feature of the environment.*

derosa pine zone, and again when the pine needle drop is complete, near the end of the year. In the demonstration, the second burn was made in March.

Fires have been dated back to A.D. 250 in the Mariposa Grove of giant sequoias in Yosemite National Park. Other dated fires in this grove occurred in 1622, 1690, 1710, 1734, 1742, 1752, 1760, 1775, 1803, 1807, and 1809. The fires here were less frequent than those in the Stanislaus National Forest because the fuels under giant sequoias are generally not as flammable as those under ponderosa pines.

A fire history of 4,500 acres of sequoia mixed-conifer forest in the Sierra Nevada was made recently by Bruce Kilgore and Dan Taylor. They studied 935 scars on 220 stumps. Fire-free intervals between 1700 and 1875 varied by habitat from five years in ponderosa pine on a dry ridge to 15–18 years in more moist sites with white fir. Fires of various sizes were found to have burned every two to three years somewhere in a given drainage. Scar records prior to 1700 suggest fairly comparable intervals. Evidence of fires diminished greatly after burning by Indians was eliminated in the early 1870s, and the records became almost nonexistent after 1900, when fire suppression became more effective. (Similarly, working in the San Bernardino Mountains in southern California, Joe R. McBride and Richard D. Laven found a fire frequency of about ten years before 1905, when fire suppression was initiated.) Most of the pre-1875 fires were small and of low intensity. Even the larger fires were usually confined to one slope or one drainage area. Intense fires that might move from crown to crown were absent in the study area.

Observations have shown that many of the low-intensity fires burn in fire scars without injuring the new wood. Because those fires would not, of course, be recorded, they could not be dated through ring counts. For this reason, studies of fire frequency from fire scars are nearly always too conservative.

In chaparral, dating of recurring fires may be difficult. However, determining when the last fire burned is easily done by studying the age of stump sprouts of trees, such as scrub oak or scrub interior live oak, scattered through the chaparral.

Plant Adaptations to Fire

Myriad plants show remarkable adaptations to fire. It is probable that many of these adaptations evolved with recurring fires over the centuries.

Listed here are the features that help trees, shrubs, and herbaceous plants adapt to low-intensity fires. Examples of plants in which these features appear are given in parentheses.

Trees
1. Thick bark (ponderosa pine)
2. Corky bark with low conductivity of heat (white fir and Douglas-fir)
3. Very hard bark (coast live oak)
4. Epicormic branching (i.e., trunk and stem sprouts) (coast redwood, big-cone Douglas-fir, and eucalyptus)
5. Basal sprouting (all oaks)
6. Serotinous cones, which may remain on the trees for many years and open after heating by fire (knobcone and some lodgepole pines)
7. Buds protected by a heavy pubescence and new growth remaining at ground level for three or four years (longleaf pine in the southeastern United States)
8. New sprouts from shallow roots (quaking aspen)
9. Very rapid early growth that enables the plant to get out of reach of low-intensity surface fires in a short time (longleaf pine after it starts upright growth)
10. Large butt swells that help prevent fuels from accumulating at the base of trees (sugar pine)
11. Casting of seeds almost yearly, thus assuring that seeds will fall on any freshly burned areas (giant sequoia)

Shrubs
1. Stump sprouting after fire (chamise and many other shrubs)
2. New shoots from rhizomes (yerba santa)
3. Heavy seed production at an early age (nonsprouting species of manzanita and ceanothus)
4. Seeds that can remain dormant for many years until fire cracks their seedcoats creating conditions favorable for germination (species of manzanita and ceanothus)

5. Reproduction by layering (Eastwood and Mexican manzanitas)

Herbaceous Plants

1. Location of growing points at ground level or below (some of the perennial grasses and sedges)
2. Sprouting of several of the perennial forbs from stems or roots (soap plant)
3. Dormancy during the dry season (pine bluegrass and purple needlegrass)
4. Burial of seeds beneath the ground by hygroscopic awns, where they are safe from fire (filarees)
5. Stiff reverse hairs on the seedcoats, which help work the seeds down close to the soil, where they are not likely to be burned (foxtail barley)

Figure 31. *Giant sequoias that reproduced in an open area after a prescribed fire in heavy debris. These trees, on Redwood Mountain in Kings Canyon National Park, are ten years old, having been retarded in height growth for several years by browsing deer.*

Figure 32. *Giant sequoia seedlings that followed a low-intensity prescribed fire. Eighty-five seedlings were counted on this one-square-foot plot. But not a single seedling will live more than one to three years because the microhabitat is not suitable for their establishment. The low-intensity fire was sufficient for seed germination but not for seedling survival. The giant sequoia needs an intense surface fire to remove litter and destroy soil pathogens in preparation for new reproduction.*

6. A good percentage of hard seeds that may be conditioned for germination by fire (some of the clovers and lupines)

Vegetation's Dependence on Fire

Some plant species and vegetation communities have become dependent on fire for seedbed preparation, seed germination, early growth of seedlings, and maintenance. Indeed, some species and communities are so dependent on fires that without them they would eventually become rare and endangered, as is now the case with giant sequoias in the Placer County Big Tree Grove.

The giant sequoia is a classic example of the need for fire for seedbed preparation. Thriving seedlings are seldom seen except in areas that have been burned. In this case, fire functions to reduce the duff (partially decomposed material) and debris, enabling the small seeds to fall on mineral soil as well as ridding the seedbed of pathogens and poisonous substances. (See Figures 31–33.)

Figure 33. *A giant sequoia in the South Grove of Calaveras Big Trees State Park in spring 1988. The tree is growing fast in a spot where a moderately intense prescribed fire burned in December 1980. After the fire, many young trees became established in this general area, near the Agassiz tree, biggest of the Calaveras sequoias. Can we say that all this rapid growth was due to the favorable habitat or was some of it due to inheritance from the Agassiz tree?*

Other plants produce seeds that have heavy coats and require fire to condition them for germination—for instance, by cracking the seedcoat, enabling the seed to imbibe water. Examples are the seeds of many chaparral shrubs and herbs, whose new seedlings may appear in great abundance after a fire.

Certain plant communities also depend on recurring fires for their continued well-being. A good example is that of ponderosa pine communities, which thrive with frequent low-intensity fires. When such fires are prevented, these communities give way to mixed conifers with large percentages of shade-tolerant white fir and incense-cedar. Many grassland communities also depend on recurring fires, and without them give way to shrubs.

Chapter Three

Wildfires

Is fire management on a collision course with disaster? Perhaps, because wildfires continue to become more intense and destructive of resources, and expenses in fire control are increasing at an astronomical rate.

William E. Towell, chairman of a fire study group for the American Forestry Association, was probably right when he said that "a fire control agency's worst enemy may be its own efficiency. The longer forests go without burning, the greater the fuel accumulation and the greater the fire hazard." That is exactly the situation we face today. Wildfire-control agencies have continually expanded and improved their fire-fighting capability through adding more year-long and seasonal personnel; providing better training; building more roads; and using more bulldozers and pumpers, airplanes and helicopters, and fire retardants. But as a counter to these developments, the fuels continually increase in volume and flammability, and the wildfire problem inexorably worsens. (See Figures 34–35.) Severe wildfires are experienced every year. The account in the following pages touches only the surface.

The Peshtigo and Hinckley Fires

To fully understand the problem of wildfires, we must go back to settlements in the Great Lakes region. Some of the early settlers there were amassing fortunes from logging operations. One of them was William B. Ogden, president of the Peshtigo

Figure 34. *A wildfire. Fires like this one, usually burning upslope or with the wind, can endanger human life, destroy timber and houses, and damage watersheds and scenic values. It has been proven that prescribed burning can be an effective means of reducing fuels and lessening the often disastrous effects of such a fire.*

Company, a booming lumber concern near Green Bay, Wisconsin. The area around Peshtigo was a green gold mine, and acre after acre was quickly cut over, the slash being left in deep piles, along with mounds of chips and sawdust. Fires in logging slash and debris from clearings were allowed to burn unattended, for they had done no great harm in the past. The year 1871 proved to be an exception, for it was the year of a great drought.

Figure 35. *Aftermath of a wildfire. A wildfire in Stanislaus National Forest in 1950 was burning 1,000 acres per hour when a sudden shower dampened the fuels, enabling fire fighters to put it out. Four years later, after the area was salvage logged, the ground is covered with slash and young plants of snow brush that came from seed stored in the soil. In another three or four years, after the dead trees fall, the shrubs will climb over the debris, and the area will become nearly impenetrable except by bulldozer. It will then pose a major fire hazard.*

The past year had been dry, but 1871 was even drier. After June 8, there was no rain for 117 days. Rangeland fires in the eastern Dakotas were moving into Wisconsin, and on September 19 a sawdust pile of the Peshtigo Company caught on fire. The fire was extinguished by company employees, but through the next week, fires of varying sizes were burning all around Peshtigo. The smoky atmosphere disturbed few people until October 7, when the sky reddened and the smoke became thick. When the fires neared the villages around Peshtigo, they exploded into a huge flash of flames. The firestorm engulfed the small village of Sugar Bush, and not a single person escaped to warn the residents of Peshtigo. The fireball roared across Peshtigo, igniting wooden buildings, wooden sidewalks, and everything else in its path that would burn. People leaped into the river whether they could swim or not as the fire moved north, east, and south simultaneously. Over 1,200 people perished in 20 short minutes.

But this catastrophe in the backwoods hardly made news. On the same day, blown by the same high wind, the Great Chicago Fire, supposedly started in straw bedding when Mrs. O'Leary's cow kicked over a lantern, destroyed most of Chicago, killing 250 to 300 people, burning 12,000 buildings, and leaving almost 100,000 persons homeless. Understandably, it received all the publicity. William Ogden pledged to help rebuild Chicago with his great resources, unaware that his Peshtigo Company and his empire had met the same fate as Chicago. It was weeks before the news of Peshtigo spread around the country, and during that time wildfires in logging slash had desolated a large section of Michigan. The total area burned in the Peshtigo Fire was 1,280,000 acres, while fires in Michigan burned 2,500,000 acres.

By the 1890s, the Lake States had been ravaged for 25 years by fires in logging slash. Hinckley, Minnesota, was no exception. The summer of 1894 was dry and hot; rainfall was only 16 percent of normal, the temperature five degrees above average, and the humidity 20 percent below average almost all summer. Slash and range fires were burning in many places. A strong wind came on September 1 and, just before noon, smoke began billowing to the west of Hinckley. Outlying settlers moved into town. Converging fires from the south and west joined at the edge of town as a 20-foot storm of fire seared the town. Though 500 people escaped by train, over 400 were trapped and killed by the flames.

Other destructive fires continued to burn in the Great Lakes region. For instance, in 1918, in eastern Minnesota, the Cloquet Fire burned 250,000 acres, and 453 people perished in the firestorm that enveloped the villages around Cloquet.

Policy of Fire Exclusion

The Peshtigo and Hinckley fires were mammoth blazes, but they were only two of the hundreds of damaging wildfires that had now burned across slash-filled, cutover forests. These desolated areas were terrible eyesores, as well as examples of very poor forestry practices. Pictures and stories of the devastation were circulated around the country, and public awareness of diminishing resources encouraged the first conservation movement in America.

In 1896 the National Academy of Sciences appointed a Forest Commission to recommend an administration and management system for the existing forest reserves and to suggest new areas that should be reserved. Two years later, Gifford Pinchot, an eastern aristocrat with European forestry training, was appointed head of the Division of Forestry. He soon began to mold a powerful, well-organized agency, which in 1901 was renamed the Bureau of Forestry (the name change perhaps being made to give the agency more clout in the Washington hierarchy). By 1905, with the passage of the Transfer Act, one of Pinchot's long-pursued goals was achieved—the transfer of the bureau from the Department of the Interior to the Department of Agriculture—and again, it got a new name, the Forest Service.

The Use Book, published in the same year for the administration and management of Forest Service lands, advocated a new policy concerning the exclusion of fire from forests. On both public and private lands, total fire exclusion was encouraged because many of the forest problems of the past had been associated with wildfires. That the wildfires were largely a result of forest fuel accumulations was not understood, and a blanket indictment against fire was issued as the official policy. It would have been better if *The Use Book* had placed emphasis on silvicultural and management practices that prevented heavy forest-fuel accumulations, but those amassings were not recognized as the main problem at that time.

The Great Idaho Fire

In 1910, severe fire weather conditions extended over much of the western United States. During that summer, many wildfires burned in the Northwest from lightning and other causes. Fire fighters had done a fine job through June and July, suppressing 3,000 small fires and 90 large ones. But their luck ran out; the extensive logging slash and long drought produced the inevitable. After two months of hot, dry weather, a ten-day spell of high winds and low humidity set the scene for the ghastly yellow sky of August 20. Starting in logging slash and pushed by strong winds, the flames soon approached firestorm intensity. The holocaust swept over more than 3 million acres of forestland in Idaho and Montana and killed 85 people before it was finally conquered, while 1,736 other fires blazed through the forests at the same time. During this dry period, some 240,000 acres burned in California. Although these fires were not quite as catastrophic as the Peshtigo and Hinckley fires, big headlines in the newspapers empowered conservationists to preach for better management. But the impact of the Great Idaho Fire also strengthened the policy that no fires be allowed in forests under any conditions for any management objective.

The Great Idaho Fire influenced Congress to pass the Weeks Act in 1911. This law allowed the government to purchase land for national forests and set up federal-state cooperation in fire control. Section 2 of the act allotted $200,000 for cooperative efforts to protect forested watersheds of navigable streams from fire. The law also stimulated individual states to enact fire legislation by requiring such legislation in each cooperating state before federal funds were granted.

The Berkeley Fire

In California, on September 17, 1923, a strong, hot, dry northeast wind quickly brought a fire out of Wildcat Canyon, precisely where I live, just over the ridge east of Berkeley, an area that is now Tilden Park. The fire spread quickly through dry grass into a large eucalyptus grove along the crest of the ridge. There, the fire burned vigorously, with high convection, through dry, oily eucalyptus leaves and bark. Suddenly it burst out into the residential area far below, apparently having reached this remote area by firebrands from the eucalyptus trees. Within 40 minutes after the first house caught fire at 2:20 P.M., burning shingles were sailing over the rooftops throughout an area one-half mile square. Within another two hours or so, 625 houses and other buildings on 60 square blocks were destroyed. Fortunately, and almost unbelievably, the flames took no human lives. At about 4:30 P.M., the strong winds began to die down and were replaced by a coastal breeze that enabled fire fighters to extinguish the blaze. One wonders what would have happened if the northeast winds had continued a while longer.

For several days before the fire, coastal fog had kept the humidity near 100 percent and temperatures around 50° to 60° F. There was no imminent danger of wildfire. But fire weather conditions can change rapidly. On the night before the fire, the fog suddenly disappeared, and by midnight the temperature had soared to 82 degrees. By dawn, the wind was blowing steadily at gale force over the crest of the hills and down toward the bay. Early risers noted that the sky was crystal clear and the air dry and full of static electricity. The stage was set. No rain had fallen on Berkeley since spring (as California summers are normally dry), and the sun-bleached grasses, further dried out by the northeast winds, burned as if they had been doused with gasoline. (See Figure 36.)

For a few years after the 1923 fire, vacant lots in Berkeley were burned each summer in an effort to keep the fire hazards at a low level, but this practice was gradually discontinued. Eventually, complacency seems to set in after all disastrous wildfires. Instead of continually working to reduce flammable fuels and the danger of wildfires, people tend to forget the potential for such fires until another wildfire occurs, and then, of course, it is too late.

California Aflame, 1955

California experiences destructive wildfires every year. One of the most spectacular occurred in the summer of 1955, a terrible fire season. A hot, dry period in late August and early Septem-

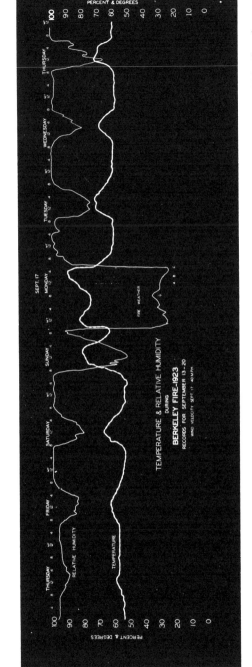

Figure 36. *Weather conditions in Berkeley immediately before, during, and after the September 17, 1923, fire that destroyed 625 homes in two hours. Note how dramatically the humidity dropped during the night of the 16th and how fast it rose soon after 4 P.M. on the 17th. Air temperature during the fire was 90° F, humidity 25 percent, and wind velocity 40 mph—a demonstration of how suddenly fire weather conditions can change. To help avoid such disasters, fuels must be managed and reduced to less hazardous conditions in urban-wildland interfaces.*

ber set the stage for 436 wildfires between August 27 and September 13. They burned more than 307,000 acres of wildlands. The state was truly aflame, and though climatic factors were instrumental in starting the multiple infernos, the large fuel accumulations in forest and chaparral caused the fires to burn beyond control. Forty-one fires ravaged more than 300 acres each. Two other fires each burned more than 75,000 acres. The conflagrations covered 141,000 acres of timber-producing lands and 166,000 acres of woodland-grass and chaparral. (See Figure 37.) The cost of control was estimated to be $3.5 million; fire damage was close to $4 million. These losses and costs were thought to be unusual. They were not, and they got worse.

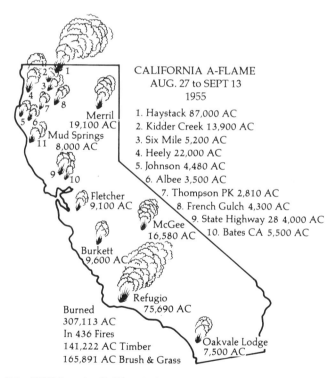

CALIFORNIA A-FLAME
AUG. 27 to SEPT 13
1955

Merril 19,100 AC
Mud Springs 8,000 AC
Fletcher 9,100 AC
McGee 16,580 AC
Burkett 9,600 AC
Refugio 75,690 AC
Oakvale Lodge 7,500 AC

1. Haystack 87,000 AC
2. Kidder Creek 13,900 AC
3. Six Mile 5,200 AC
4. Heely 22,000 AC
5. Johnson 4,480 AC
6. Albee 3,500 AC
7. Thompson PK 2,810 AC
8. French Gulch 4,300 AC
9. State Highway 28 4,000 AC
10. Bates CA 5,500 AC

Burned 307,113 AC
In 436 Fires
141,222 AC Timber
165,891 AC Brush & Grass

Figure 37. *Wildfires in California in 1955. The many fires in a short time that were burning under dry, windy conditions made fire control extremely difficult. Cost of control and damage was estimated to be about $7.5 million. The cost of restoration, if it is ever done, will amount to millions more.*

California Aflame, 1970

Inevitably, wildfires in California became ever more difficult to suppress, as well as more destructive of resources: the volume and flammability of wildland fuels continued to increase; and there were more houses to be protected and more people to get fires started in one way or another. In 1970, between September 15 and November 15, a period of severe fire weather conditions, 1,260 fires burned 600,000 acres plus 885 homes. Fourteen lives were lost. Suppression and damage were estimated at $233 million.

The most widespread conflagration was the Laguna Fire of 175,000 acres in San Diego County. Then rated the second largest fire ever to occur in California—being topped only by the Matilija Fire of 1932, which had burned 219,000 acres in the Los Padres National Forest—it started in the early morning of September 26, when a strong Santa Ana wind blew a tree across a power line. The hot line started a series of small fires in dry grass. These spread quickly into young timber and heavy brush. Very soon the wind was gusting up to 70 miles per hour, the humidity got down to 7 percent, the temperatures up to 95° F. When the fire started, air tankers made a single series of chemical retardant drops and then were grounded for the remainder of the day because of high winds and severe air turbulence. The fire spotted far ahead and covered 3,000 acres per hour for 48 hours. Fire reports said little or nothing about the volumes or ages of fuels through which the fires burned—information that could have been the most significant part of the reports.

A much smaller, but terribly destructive fire had occurred four days earlier, in the Berkeley-Oakland hills. September 22 started as another one of those crystal-clear days, with the air full of static electricity. The humidity was low and the fuels were crackling dry. Around 10 A.M., a fire started in dry grass and brush alongside the Fish Ranch Road. Fanned by a northeast wind, it quickly moved up the moderately steep slope and soon entered a residential area. Covering 204 acres, it destroyed 37 homes and damaged six others. It is generally believed that the fire was deliberately set, but the accused arsonist was acquitted in court.

Fortunately, the wind that day subsided fast. At 8 A.M. its velocity was estimated to be 40 miles per hour. When the flames broke out, it was blowing at about 15 mph. And by noon it was measured at 4 mph on the ground, but high in the atmosphere a coastal breeze was now moving the smoke inland over the burned area. Again, one wonders what further devastation would have occurred had the initial strong wind continued blowing all day.

When the 1970 series of wildfires reached its peak on September 28, some 19,500 professional fire fighters and 500 separate departments and agencies from all over the country were involved in fire fighting in California. But this was not the last series of exceptionally destructive wildfires in the state.

California Aflame, 1977

The last week of July 1977 was the beginning of a critical wildfire situation. First, the Middle Fire in the Angeles National Forest burned 3,800 acres. It was followed by one of the worst personal-property damage fires in the history of the state. On July 26, a young man was flying a kite near Santa Barbara in the Los Padres National Forest when strong gusts of wind carried the kite into high-voltage power lines. From this entanglement, sparks fell to the ground, igniting a fire that was fanned by strong winds. It eventually destroyed 250 homes at the edge of the city. This fire, like the Berkeley Fire, burned through an area of eucalyptus, where it became very intense, with high convection; it defied early control.

The wildfire situation became extremely critical during the first ten days of August because dry-storm lightning strikes set nearly 1,200 fires from south of Monterey to the Oregon border. Some 970 forest fires burned 263,000 acres and destroyed 361 million board feet of timber. Replacement costs for timber and watershed damage were estimated at $253 million. During those ten days the Forest Service encountered 449 fires, which burned 137,000 acres, and the California Department of Forestry, 521 fires, which burned 126,000 acres. The devastation occurred not because fire weather during this time was particularly severe, but because there were so many fires at one time in voluminous and highly flammable fuels, plus dense smoke that hampered fire-fighting activities.

As with the wildfires in 1970, an enormous amount of man-power and equipment was made available for fire fighting. As many as 10,000 professional fire fighters were on the fire lines. Fire crews were flown in from states as far away as Florida, Alabama, and New Hampshire.

The Marble Cone Fire was the worst during this period. It blackened 176,000 acres and became the second largest in California history, replacing the Laguna Fire of 1970 for that dubious honor. At one time, the suppression force for the Marble Cone Fire alone included 5,700 people, 65 bulldozers, 15 helicopters, and 14 air tankers. (The cost per day of running such an operation is overwhelming, soaring into millions of dollars.) Control of the fire was very difficult because of heavy, flammable fuels that averaged 40 to 50 tons, but reached up to 90 tons, per acre. Much of the fuel was dead material created by breakage of old chaparral plants from a severe snow-ice storm in 1974. Furthermore, an inversion layer for several days held smoke near the ground and completely closed down all air operations. The smoke extended all the way to Salt Lake City.

Other spectacular and destructive wildfires in early August were the Scarface Fire, 86,000 acres in the Modoc National Forest; the Hog Fire, 61,400 acres in the Klamath National Forest; and the Mt. Diablo Fire, 6,000 acres in Mt. Diablo State Park.

California Aflame, 1987

The worst siege of wildfires ever to occur in California started on August 29, 1987, when lightning struck in the Stanislaus National Forest in the mid-Sierras. Over the next seven days 12,000 more strikes were recorded, igniting a landscape of heavy flammable fuels. The fuels had been accumulating for up to 100 years and were tinder-dry. Some of the fires went out on their own; others were caught by initial attack crews. But many others were contained only with great difficulty under dangerous conditions. The last fire was controlled 50 days after the first one started. The toll: more than 700,000 incinerated acres, most of which were in national forests. Of this vast acreage, 550,000

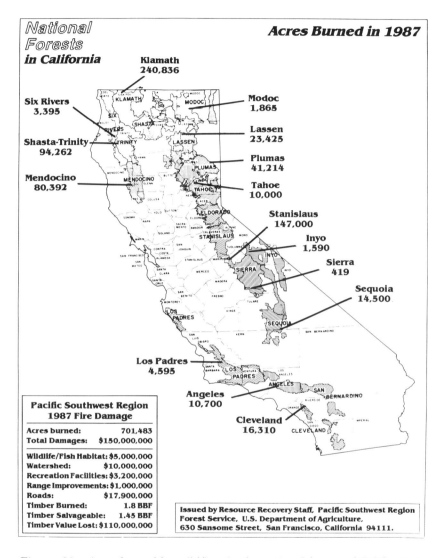

National Forests in California

Acres Burned in 1987

Klamath
240,836

Six Rivers
3,395

Shasta-Trinity
94,262

Mendocino
80,392

Modoc
1,865

Lassen
23,425

Plumas
41,214

Tahoe
10,000

Stanislaus
147,000

Inyo
1,590

Sierra
419

Sequoia
14,500

Los Padres
4,595

Angeles
10,700

Cleveland
16,310

Pacific Southwest Region 1987 Fire Damage	
Acres burned:	701,483
Total Damages:	$150,000,000
Wildlife/Fish Habitat:	$5,000,000
Watershed:	$10,000,000
Recreation Facilities:	$3,200,000
Range Improvements:	$1,000,000
Roads:	$17,900,000
Timber Burned:	1.8 BBF
Timber Salvageable:	1.45 BBF
Timber Value Lost:	$110,000,000

Issued by Resource Recovery Staff, Pacific Southwest Region Forest Service, U.S. Department of Agriculture, 630 Sansome Street, San Francisco, California 94111.

Figure 38. *Acres burned by wildfires in the national forests of California in 1987 and the cost of damage to resources.* Note: *These data are only for the national forests and do not include the fires outside them. (From "Up from the Ashes," a report issued by the Forest Service in April 1988.)*

acres were classed as commercial timber–producing lands. (See Figure 38.)

But California was not the only victim: the same series of storms set hundreds of fires in Oregon, Washington, and Idaho.

Fighting the fires was a mammoth job. Up to 19,000 fire fighters were on firelines. Containing just the Stanislaus fires of some 147,000 acres took 15 days, 5,000 people, 378 engines, 141 bulldozers, 100 water tenders, 12 air tankers, and 11 helicopters.

The fires did incalculable damage. Ten fire fighters lost their lives; 38 homes and 100 recreational facilities burned; 274 miles of trails, 63 archeological sites, and 155 miles of riparian habitat were damaged; 100,000 acres of forest plantations burned; $1 million of range improvements were incinerated; and 1.9 billion board feet of timber were blackened.

The estimated cost of controlling the fires in California was $160 million, and the longtime recovering costs are expected to be another $150 million. But these figures may change as more data become available.

The fires were blamed almost entirely on lightning, which set so many fires in a short time, and on dry weather. Nothing was said about the fuels that had been building up during the many years of fire suppression. This lapse is unfortunate as it was the heavy fuels that made the fires so difficult to control and so damaging to our wildland resources. I feel certain that a vigorous program of prescribed burning in the understory of ponderosa pine could have prevented this holocaust. The same argument applies to the catastrophic fire in Yellowstone National Park in 1988: it was the tragic payment that nature sooner or later exacts for human attempts at fire suppression.

The Wildfire-Flood Cycle

We are well aware that intense wildfires can kill people, destroy homes, and cost millions of dollars to control. But that is not all they can do. When the protective ground cover is nearly all removed, as it often is by intense wildfire, water runoff and soil erosion are sometimes severe. The amount depends not only on the intensity of the fire and cover removal, but on the kind of soil and vegetation, steepness and length of slope, storm character, and depth of the nonwettable soil layer. In some cases, the effects are long-lasting.

The wildfire-flood cycle can be particularly severe on some of the steep chaparral slopes of unconsolidated soils in southern California. Following the Middle Fire in the Angeles National Forest in July 1977, floods in February—with water 20 feet high carrying large boulders and tons of debris and mud—destroyed the mountain resort community of Hidden Springs, killing 13 people. Would this have happened if the 3,800 acres of watershed had been prescribe-burned in fragments in early spring over a period of years? We don't know, because this alternative to wildfire has not been studied enough yet. But it must be noted that not all wildfires cause accelerated water runoff and soil erosion.

Predicting Holocausts

Even under the best of wildland management practices, the wildfire problem will not diminish quickly, nor will it ever disappear completely. Natural features of the environment will see to that. As pointed out earlier, certain features invite the rapid spread of intense fires: favorable conditions for abundant plant growth in the winter and spring; long summers of extremely low precipitation; very dry fuels; low humidity, high temperatures, and occasional strong winds; and steep and rugged topography in many places, largely inaccessible to fire fighters on the ground. Furthermore, an increasing number of people continually cause more fires to get started in one way or another. Incendiaries are on the increase. Of the 1,237 people-caused fires per year in California's national forests from 1974 to 1978, arson was the number one cause in five of the 18 forests. When large fires are burning, arsonists are very often out setting more fires. A discouraging situation.

Given these conditions, another severe wildfire will undoubtedly soon take place, most likely in heavy, flammable fuels during an extremely dry, windy period. Yet, though we can't do much about topography and weather conditions, two of the principal determinants of fire behavior, we certainly can do a lot about fuels, the third determinant. We can modify and reduce them so that wildfires are less intense, more easily controlled, and not so destructive.

Several approaches to fuels reduction have been proposed or undertaken: rotational prescribed burning to create mosaics of younger-age classes and reduce the amount of dead fuels, construction of fuel breaks, and development of various fuel types—for example, converting certain areas of chaparral to grass.

Fire-fighting techniques and ground equipment are not adequate for conflagration control and the potential for control through air power is not great either. The use of air tankers on conflagration fires is beset with difficulties. The hazard of flying low over rough terrain and in turbulent winds is so great that on some fires it may preclude any use of aircraft. And even under favorable conditions, air tankers do not always provide an efficient method of fire-retardant application. On many spot fires and deep, ragged fire fronts, it is not always possible to deliver the extremely large amounts of fire retardants required for any significant effect on fire behavior.

Admittedly, many of the advanced fire-fighting techniques are effective on fires burning under low-hazard conditions, but in conflagrations, they are not highly effective. Overall and in the long run, they may even do more harm than good, since putting out small fires, burning under low-hazard conditions, tends to add to the overall buildup of fuels and their flammability.

Knowing that heavy flammable fuels contribute greatly to the severity of wildfire behavior, one can detect hundreds of places in California where the potential for conflagration fires is extremely high. Some of these are in the interfaces between town and country, and others are remote from population centers.

One interface area, for example, is the Berkeley-Oakland hills, where a wildfire burning in strong east or northeast winds could be vastly more severe than the Berkeley Fire of September 1923. Conceivably, many people could be trapped and killed if caught in a traffic jam on the narrow and crooked streets. Panoramic Way, above the university stadium, is one of the main streets in that area and is so crooked that even a small fire engine cannot go up it without backing up to make some of the sharp turns. It is also so narrow that two cars cannot pass if cars are parked along the street.

Elsewhere in the Berkeley-Oakland hills, the fuels of tall dry grass, coastal sage scrub, eucalyptus bark and leaves, and Monterey pine and coast live oak are critically dense in Tilden Park, the upper hills of the university campus, and surrounding areas. These fuels can be reduced and modified to lessen the potential for a conflagration. A first procedure would be to completely burn and clean in the understory of all for-

Figure 39. *Specimens of red shank growing in eastern San Diego County. This plant freely exfoliates its bark, which accumulates at its base. The ribbon-like debris is resinous and highly flammable.*

ested areas, including eucalyptus, pines, coast live oaks, and redwoods.

Typical of a remote area with conflagration potential is the Agua Tibia wilderness in the Palomar district of the Cleveland National Forest. Located about 50 miles north of San Diego and 75 miles southeast of Los Angeles, it covers 15,934 acres. (See Figure 39.) But since boundaries alone have little bearing on the spread of conflagration wildfires, a fast-moving fire into or out of the wilderness could cover thousands of additional acres, including perhaps Palomar Mountain State Park, Heise County Park, and portions of Cuyamaca Rancho State Park, all depending on where a fire starts and the direction of a strong, dry wind.

The Agua Tibia wilderness is mountainous and cut by many deep canyons. The slopes are covered by fragile soils supporting a plant cover of dense chaparral, while the higher ridge tops and peaks are capped with stands of conifers. Because a significant portion of the wilderness has not burned in the past 100 years, there is much dead material. Actually, I have never seen taller manzanita or larger volumes of chaparral fuels than those here. A land and resource management plan published in 1986 states that this wilderness will be prescribe-burned to restore or maintain natural conditions. It cannot be done too soon.

Chapter Four

Prescribed Burning in Historical Perspective

That wildfires should be prevented or suppressed and their damage minimized has been heartily accepted by everyone concerned with wildland resources. But the 1905 Forest Service policy encouraging fire exclusion from both public and private forest lands was another matter. It caused a very long period of controversy and dissension during which many professional foresters suffered a loss of credibility.

Although a good deal of the information in this chapter refers to the past, a knowledge of the history of prescribed burning should be of value in present and future planning of fire management practices.

Control Burning in the Piney Woods

Much of the early-day controversy about prescribed, or control, burning centered on the piney woods of the southern and southeastern United States. Ashley Schiff, of the School of Public Administration at the University of Southern California, discussed the situation well in his 1962 book *Fire and Water: Scientific Heresy in the Forest Service*. Having myself worked in the piney woods from 1940 to 1947, I became acquainted with the local fire problems and with most of the people mentioned in Schiff's book.

The Fire Ecology of Longleaf Pine

The piney woods is a vast forest area extending from North Carolina to eastern Texas. The principal conifers are pines: longleaf, slash, loblolly, and shortleaf. At the time of the first settlements, longleaf pine was "king" of the whole domain: widespread, abundant, and superb for both timber and turpentine.

For thousands of years, fires set by lightning or by Indians had periodically burned through the piney woods. The longleaf must have flourished under those conditions. In a sense, the control burns of later times were to play about the same role in the forests as lightning fires had performed naturally for centuries.

For some 200 years prior to the fire exclusion policy, farmers with cattle had annually set fires in the forests to get rid of pine needles and old grass and to freshen the forage; they had seen that their cattle preferred to graze burned areas and that they made good weight gains there. Each year the farmers set fires in January or February and let them spread through the forests. The fires were light because the annual burning in the cool of winter, along with grazing, prevented the buildup of fuels.

Nevertheless, many foresters regarded the long-established custom as terribly destructive. They maintained that, rather than helping grazing, burning hurt the forage plants and lowered their value and that it was also harmful to longleaf pine reproduction and growth. Forestry personnel referred to the practice as indiscriminate burning.

True, foresters had noted that longleaf pine did not reproduce well in logged areas protected from fire, but they were not especially worried; they thought that if fire and hogs were kept out of the forests and ample seed trees left, nature itself would restore longleaf to its primeval state. However, that did not happen. Clearly, something more was needed. That something was fire, upon which longleaf is highly dependent to remove forest debris and prepare the soil for seed reception. The longleaf pine is well adapted to low-intensity fires. The seeds germinate in the fall soon after they drop. During the first year, the seedling is very sensitive—any fire in January or February, after germination, will kill the seedlings. But by the next January or February, nearly all the seedlings will survive a fire.

The early growth of longleaf pine is unique. For three to five years, the seedling does not grow upright, but instead develops a strong root system; the foliage stays in what is known as the "grass stage." Needles arise from the root crown, and if fire removes them, a new crop is produced. After the root crown is about one-half inch thick—three to five years after seed germination—upright growth begins and is rapid for three or four years. During this brief period of fast growth, the tree is very sensitive to fire. Once the tree is five or six feet tall, any damage from low-intensity fires is negligible. After the upright growth, the buds of winter are covered by a heavy, compact pubescence, which protects them from fire. In fact, wintertime fires may be intense enough to kill all needles, but new ones arise from the buds that were protected by the pubescence. Such fires may retard growth, but they do not kill the trees.

Thus, in keeping with the distinctive fire ecology of longleaf pine, the steps in control burning are as follows:

1. Use fire in the winter ahead of a good seed crop to prepare the soil for seed reception.
2. Exclude fire for 15 months after seed germination.
3. Control-burn three or four years after seed germination to remove any grass that might be shading the seedlings.
4. Exclude fire for three or four years while the seedlings are making rapid growth.
5. Continue control burning about every three years to retard understory oaks and brush and keep down wildfire hazards.

The fire exclusion policy failed in its aim to stop the annual burning, and it was only prescribed burning, such as that just described, that years later made it possible to break the custom and improve on it. By that time, as we shall see, research had proven that burning was indeed beneficial for longleaf pine reproduction and growth, grazing, wildlife habitat, control of understory oaks and brush, prevention of brown spot disease on longleaf pine seedlings, and reduction of wildfire hazards. Further, the soil, even under annual burning, showed some chemical improvement, probably because nitrogen-fixing legumes increased with burning. (The soil, however, showed slight compaction, perhaps from the force of raindrops or from the hoofs of grazing animals, so that it was not well aerated and lost some of its water-absorbing capacity.)

Demise of the Fire Exclusion Policy

The prolonged reluctance of many foresters to acknowledge burning as beneficial in longleaf pine—as, in fact, essential for the perpetuation of the species—is especially curious because the historical record offered considerable evidence of the usefulness of the practice. The role of fire in maintaining longleaf pine had long been observed. Early travelers had recorded their observations on the burning practices of Indians and early settlers. Perhaps the first indication that fires might create conditions favorable to longleaf pine came from Charles Lyell, an English geologist, who said in 1849:

These hills were covered with longleaf pines and the large proportion they bear to hardwoods is said to have been increased by the Indian practice of burning the grass; the bark of the oaks and other kinds of hardwoods being more combustible, and more easily injured by fire, than most of the fir tribe. Everywhere the seedlings of the longleaved pine were coming up in such numbers that one might have supposed the ground to have been sown by them.

Forty years later, in 1889, Mrs. Ellen Call Long of Tallahassee, whose background I don't know but who must have been an extremely perceptive woman, wrote:

The annual burning of the wooded regions of the South is the prime cause and preserver of the grand forests of *Pinus palustris* [longleaf pine] to be found there; but for the effects of these burnings . . . the maritime pine belt would soon disappear and give place to a jungle of hardwood and deciduous trees. . . . The statute books of almost every southern state contain enactments prohibitory of setting fires to the woods, and severe penalties are attached to violation of the law. There may be sound reason for such legislation, since great loss of property often results from burning fences and buildings. But viewed from a forestry standpoint we believe the total abolition of forest fire in the South would mean the annihilation of her grand lumbering pineries.

Before 1907, no Forest Service official had ever sanctioned in print any use of fire in the piney woods. In that year, however, T. T. Munger, forest assistant and later director of the Pacific Northwest Forest Experiment Station, showed alarm over the potential extinction of longleaf pine. He submitted an excellent report to his superiors that contained several proposals for securing adequate longleaf pine restocking. One of his proposals advocated fire plus clear-cutting, with provision for leaving ample seed trees. He saw this method as entirely practical, cheap, suited to the habits of longleaf pine, and requiring no special skill. As he explained:

A lumberman owns a large tract of longleaf pine land which he is going to log during the next twenty or thirty years. When he sees by the small cones on the trees that a good seed year is coming, he purposely burns over, under careful supervision, the land which he is planning to log during the next five or six years. This fire will prepare the soil for the reception of the seed, which when it falls in the autumn, should germinate even in the light shade of the old trees and form a carpet of seedlings through this section of the forest. The owner then installs an efficient system of fire protection so that the seedlings which start after the good seed year will not be killed. After the seed is shed from the trees, the lumberman proceeds to log this section, cutting everything merchantable, only taking reasonable precautions not to destroy the little pine seedlings. . . . The fire protection on this section will be continued until the young growth is past the age when it can be killed by fire, which is about 10 years of age. Thereafter it may be advisable to burn over the tract each year during the wettest part of the year, so that the pine straw will not collect for years and be the source of a serious conflagration when it does catch fire.

In a similar vein, Anton T. Boison, acting chief of silvics in the Forest Service, replying in 1907 to a letter of inquiry about fire, wrote:

Fire is of course the great enemy of the longleaf pine, and protection against fire is an absolutely essential first step toward securing a new crop. Rightly used, however, it may be of considerable assistance in securing new growth. If an area which is to be logged is burnt over just before the last seed year, thus destroying the leaf litter and exposing the mineral soil, favorable conditions for germination will then be secured and large quantities of seedlings should result. If fire is then excluded and the logging done with moderate care, enough of the seedlings should be left to form a good second crop. Seed trees should, however, always be left.

Although both Munger's and Boison's suggestions concerning the use of fire were excellent, they were never accepted by higher authority.

Later on, the initiative in assessing beneficial uses of fire fell largely on nongovernmental personnel and on a few government foresters who dared express their opinions unofficially. An early-day researcher on control burning in the piney woods was H. H. Chapman, professor of forestry at Yale University. He started research on the role of fire in longleaf pine silviculture in 1907 (the same year Munger and Boison had stated their case). Soon thereafter, he recommended control burning in the fall preceding a seed year and again after the period of fire danger to young trees—that is, after the trees were five or six feet tall. In reports to the Forest Service, he showed diplomacy and tried to make clear that fire exclusion was absolutely mandatory between germination and the later resistant stage. Chapman suggested that species survival required modification of local customs, not their eradication. He maintained that fire always had been and always would be an element in longleaf forests. The problem, therefore, was not how fire could be eliminated, but how it could be controlled so as, first, to secure reproduction, and second, to prevent the accumulation of litter and reduce the danger of a really disastrous blaze. In 1926, almost 20 years after his research began, he published a bulletin recommending control burning in longleaf pine on a three-year rotation basis to establish pine stands, suppress competing vegetation, reduce fuel accumulations, and rid the stands of a needle blight called brown spot disease. This disease is active while the longleaf seedling is in the grass stage, so a surface fire at that time can effectively curb its harmful effects.

Between 1911 and 1914, Ronald Harper, a botanist with the Alabama Polytechnic Institute, wrote a series of articles on "A

Defense of Forest Fires." In these, he pointed out the relationships between longleaf pine and fire. Like Chapman, he tried
to be diplomatic and therefore condemned the so-called pro-
miscuous burning, but pointed out:

At the present time most of the fires in the pineywoods are set purposely, to burn off the grass and improve the grazing. This practice
has been repeatedly denounced by persons who have spent most of
their lives outside of the longleaf pine regions, but really the only just
criticism of it that can be made is that it is done too often; oftener than
nature intended, one might say.

Not being a member of the forestry profession, Harper was described as a "car-window botanist," and his arguments were
dismissed as of little value.

Among others who supported Chapman were James W. Toumey of Yale and Austin Cary of Harvard and Yale, both pro-
fessors of forestry. They, too, wanted to be diplomatic, so they
tried to dissociate themselves from those who burned promis-
cuously: untimely and repeated fires, they acknowledged, were
the archenemy of all southern pines. But control burning, they
pointed out, was a different matter. Toumey explained that fire
could be both a blessing and a curse; that regulation, not exclusion, most suited the requirements of longleaf pine. Fire, more
than anything else, appeared to be the silvicultural tool that determined the future stand. Cary, a forest engineer, believed
that any policy not in harmony with nature's laws was fore-
doomed to failure. In discussing policy, he said:

In the first place, I think it bad policy to manage a tract of government
timber land as large and conspicuous as this in any other than what is
believed to be the most effective and business-like fashion, such as
the other men can safely follow. Secondly, it seems to me a very desirable thing for the management of the National Forests to be pleas-
ant and friendly, easy to do business with, not rigid or sticking un-
necessarily for things the local people don't believe in. . . . It has
seemed to me that it would be wisest not to face this state of things
with rigid and universal opposition to the custom.

Cary, like Chapman, was convinced that fire could be used
beneficially in longleaf pine, but because of professional pride,

he tried to avoid bringing his argument to public attention. He wanted to keep the controversy within the professional ranks.

The Roberts Research Plots.   Meanwhile, the Forest Service, anxious to prove with scientific evidence that annual burning was detrimental to the growth of longleaf pine, began an experiment. Wilbur Matoon and W. W. Ashe, USFS research personnel, divided a one-acre plot into four sections: the first section was burned annually and grazed, the second was burned annually and ungrazed, the third was unburned and grazed, and the fourth was unburned and ungrazed. These were known as the Roberts Plots. They were well stocked with longleaf pine that had reproduced after the 1913 seed crop.

For several years, annual burning slowed growth because of foliage scorching, much to the delight of those people who had been preaching the detrimental effects of annual burning. However, a few years later, when the trees became taller and scorching less severe, those on the annually burned plots began to outgrow the ones on the protected plots. Interestingly, when this happened, all talk about the greater growth on the protected plots quietly stopped.

I had the pleasure of seeing the Roberts Plots in 1941 in company with E. L. Demmon, director of the Southern Forest Experiment Station and a strong supporter of research on the role of fire in the piney woods. At that time, the trees on the annually burned plots were four to five feet taller than those on the protected plots—and the difference was easily discernible.

The Dixie Crusaders and Other Diehards.   In 1927, the American Forestry Association (AFA) began a three-year educational campaign to rid the piney woods of fire. It issued a pamphlet, "Woods Fires—Everyone's Enemy," and recruited teams of young men called Dixie Crusaders to roll through the piney woods broadcasting the slogans "Stop Wild Fires," "Growing Children Need Growing Trees," and "Everybody Loses When Timber Burns." (See Figure 40.) They covered 300,000 miles, disseminating 2 million pieces of literature and showing motion pictures 5,200 times.

Figure 40. *Early fire prevention poster featuring the "red demon." The friendly face of Smokey the Bear reveals a very different, and perhaps better, attempt to win public compliance.*

During those years, the Forest Service endeavored to weed out from its publications all references to any beneficial uses of fire. In fact, control burning had become an outlaw in the forests. Complete protection was increasingly touted as the desirable and ultimate goal. Fire, man's universal enemy, would be attacked with equal vigor on all fronts.

The Great Idaho Fire of 1910 was cited to illustrate the need for absolute protection. But it was that fire that influenced Chapman to stress the fire protection aspects of control burning. And some Forest Service personnel were beginning to take the same tack. For example, Inman Eldredge, first supervisor of the Florida National Forest, dared suggest special consideration for the fire problems of his domain. He thought that unusually heavy fuel accumulations and scrub oak in the forests amply justified control burning as a hazard-reduction measure. These arguments were discredited, however. I remember Eldredge as a man of great personality and persuasive powers. I was at a large meeting of foresters in Atlanta when the volatile subject of control burning came up, as it always did at such gatherings. For a few minutes, fistfights were imminent. Then Eldredge slowly rose to his feet and said, "Fellows, we are talking about two different things; some of us are talking about indiscriminate fires and others are talking about burning with skills and for a purpose; it can be called prescribed burning." By the time he finished, tempers had cooled and discussions continued smoothly.

McNeill, Mississippi, Grazing Study.   In 1923, R. D. Forbes, director of the Southern Forest Experiment Station and a strong opponent of prescribed burning, wanted proof that fires are detrimental both to forest range grazing and to longleaf pine reproduction. Accordingly, an experiment was started at McNeill, Mississippi. Responsibility for the research fell to three government agencies: the Forest Service, the Bureau of Animal Industry, and the Bureau of Plant Industry. The research plan was quite similar to that of the Roberts Plots. Two 150-acre pastures were fenced, and in each pasture a plot of ten acres was also fenced. Thus, there were four research plots: two of 140 acres each and two of ten acres each. The first plot was annually burned and grazed, the second was unburned and grazed, the third was annually burned and ungrazed, and the fourth was completely protected. It is important to note that, in setting up the experiment, the researchers ignored Chapman's suggestion that burning be done about every three years.

After six years of data gathering, S. W. Greene of the Bureau of Animal Industry reported that cattle on the annually burned and grazed pasture made better gains than those on the protected pasture, the differences amounting to 32 to 62 pounds per animal. This weight advantage, he contended, thoroughly verified the cattlemen's argument that cattle do better on burned ranges.

Greene also saw that fire could be beneficial in regenerating longleaf pine. Fascinated by this observation, he wrote an article spunkily titled "The Forest That Fire Made." The manuscript was strongly rejected by the AFA. Unlike the foresters, Greene was not willing to pussyfoot about facts, so he discussed newspaper publication with a cousin who was the general manager of the Associated Press. When the AFA learned about this, it immediately informed Greene that *American Forests*, the magazine of the AFA, would publish his article. It appeared in print in October 1931, with this preface:

In this article, the author raises questions that will be warmly controverted. His conclusions that the longleaf forests of the South are the result of long years of grass fires and that continued fires are essential to the perpetuation of the species as a type will come as a startling and revolutionary theory to readers schooled to the belief that fire in any form is the arch-enemy of forests and forestry. Professional foresters accustomed to distinguish sharply between indiscriminate woods burning and carefully controlled, intelligently directed and limited use of fire for specific silvicultural ends will be less startled, though they may dissent in varying degree from the particular views expounded.

Mr. Greene, it should be pointed out, is not a forester. For the past fifteen years, he has represented the Bureau of Animal Industry at the Coastal Plains Experiment Station at McNeill, Mississippi, in the study of the effect of ground fires upon forage production in the South. For a number of years, his work has been in cooperation with the United States Forest Service in its study of the influence of fire upon forest growth. His conclusions, therefore, while not official expressions of the government, have been arrived at through study and observation at first hand.

In publishing the article, *American Forests* does not vouch for the accuracy of Mr. Greene's conclusions. It does, however, believe them worthy of consideration. It is unalterably opposed to the unrestrained and irresponsible burning of the woods that now characterizes the South. Controlled burning intelligently applied and practiced where proven beneficial is an altogether different thing. Regulated burning under certain conditions and limitations may have an important place in the management of longleaf pine forests. The Forest Service has been studying fire and forestry in the South for the past ten years and in view of Mr. Greene's contentions, the facts so far as determined by it should be brought to light as quickly as possible.

In the meantime, the American people, so prone to be careless with fire in the woods, must distinguish between the meaning of controlled and uncontrolled forest fires. The difference is as great as that between the subdued fire in the hearth that warms the home and the devastating flames that reduce the home to ashes. Discussion of the subject must not lessen the public's regard for care with fire in the woods.—Editor.

But most government officials remained unswayed. As a result of his article and subsequent frank talk presenting facts and encouraging control burning in longleaf pine, Greene was eased out of his position with the Bureau of Animal Industry in 1936. I was told that he then went into the pet food business and became wealthy.

The McNeill studies were finally published in June 1939 as USDA Bulletin 683. It was the first official recognition by the Forest Service of the merits of control burning in longleaf pine. After the manuscript was submitted, it took a full six years for it to appear in print. During that period there was a large increase in pine seedlings in the annually burned and grazed pasture because grazing had so reduced the fuels that the fires were not uniform in coverage; not every square foot burned each year. If the fires had completely covered each area, every pine seedling would have been killed in the first control burn following germination.

Bobwhite Quail Studies.   By 1920, many Southern plantation owners, convinced that fires were destructive, stopped all burning. By 1923, the bobwhite quail population had declined to such a point that a meeting was convened in New York to find out why quail hunting had become so poor. The outcome of this meeting was the formation of a Cooperative Quail Study Investigation. Herbert L. Stoddard, Sr., was chosen to head the study under the direction of the U.S. Biological Survey. Within a year, he saw that the lack of control burning was one of the primary problems, and he recommended to plantation owners that they go back to regular burning. The quail apparently benefited from control burning because fire not only got rid of the debris that hindered the quail's foraging and movements, but also favored the germination of the seeds of leguminous plants, the seeds being part of the game bird's diet.

Stoddard's studies with the Biological Survey began in March of 1924 and continued until the publication in 1931 of his book *The Bobwhite Quail: Its Habits, Preservation, and Increase*, which was a further disturbance to those who had been preaching fire exclusion.

Stoddard experienced great difficulty in getting the manuscript of his study approved for publication. He had to rewrite and water down the fire chapter five times before it was finally accepted. The reason: In those days, a manuscript originating in one government agency had to go through channels to be approved in other related agencies before being published. Fortunately, at least in the Biological Survey there was no opposition—just the contrary. Stoddard had the full backing of W. L. McAtee, head of the Division of Food Habits Research, in which the bobwhite quail investigation was organized. After 1931, a new cooperative quail study association was organized and financed under private auspices.

Soil Studies.   In 1934, the results of a study by Frank Heyward and R. M. Barnette appeared as Florida Agricultural Experiment Station Bulletin 265, under the title "The Effect of Frequent Fires on the Chemical Composition of Forest Soils in the Longleaf Pine Region." This study demolished the widely accepted belief that fires in the piney woods exhaust soil fertility. The researchers reported that soils subjected to frequent fires contain less acid and possess higher percentages of replaceable calcium and total nitrogen, as well as more organic matter, than the soils of unburned areas. Some of this difference may be due both to the greater abundance of leguminous nitrogen-fixing plants that usually follow fires in that area and to the greater quantity of fibrous grass roots decaying in the soil.

Protective Burning.   A rash of severe wildfires on Forest Service lands in 1932 and again in 1934 caused many high-ranking government foresters in administration to question the wisdom of practicing fire exclusion. Among these were Forest Supervisors Inman Eldredge, Raymond Conarro, and Frank Albert and Assistant Regional Foresters A. C. Shaw, C. F. Evans, and Arthur Hartman.

Frustrations in fighting wildfires persuaded these foresters of the merits of control burning. Their view was reinforced when holocausts struck the national forests in 1941. The Impassable Bay fire in the Osceola National Forest in Florida almost completely destroyed 25,000 acres of its finest pole stands of longleaf and slash pine. The rate of spread and intensity of flames were described by Hartman in these words:

They just plumb surprised our organization. The area was mostly 8-year-old rough or more. It could be said that the Service not having previously met such conditions had not recognized the potentials and was not ready in thinking, equipment or techniques to control a fire under these conditions.

Conflagrations recurred the very next year and then the next—those in 1943 leading to new regional records in forest acreage loss and resultant monetary damage. It became obvious that in Forest Service areas more government timber was being lost to wildlife than was being produced. In other words, forestry officials were playing a losing game. Ever since the Cogdell blaze of 1934 in Georgia, many private timberland owners had been practicing control burning. In the winter of 1942, William Oettmeier, president of Superior Pine Products Company in Fargo, Georgia, alone burned 30,000 acres. To save face with such companies, government policy reversal seemed necessary.

A Change in Policy.   Convinced that there must be a change in policy regarding control burning, Joe Kircher, the regional forester, invited Lyle Watts, chief of the Forest Service, to come south and personally survey fire conditions. Watts accepted the invitation and, shortly after arriving, witnessed the effects of the frequent holocausts. Considerably distressed, he wrote to Supervisor Frank Albert:

I assure you that I will not soon forget the ten days that I spent with Regional Forester Kircher and others in the deep South. Certainly I will not forget that in Florida there is an acute fire problem and that adequate heavy equipment is one of the essential requirements for getting on top of the job. I must admit that control burning has me somewhat confused. However, the way that the big fire substantiated your own judgment of things to happen, within a week after you explained it to me, lends a lot of emphasis to your own ideas. I hope that you and Kircher are able to work out a program designed to get at answers which the land administrators must have.

Shortly thereafter, Pat Thompson, recently appointed fire control chief in the Washington office, joined Kircher in starting a drive for acceptance of control burning. Before writing a tentative directive, they arranged for Arthur Nelson, chief of Timber Management, and Walt Dutton, chief of the Division of Grazing, to tour the South. Meanwhile, C. F. Evans sought to line up state foresters, some of whom had strongly opposed any efforts at control burning. Evans circulated among state foresters this letter from a county agricultural agent:

Looking back over the past 26 years, I have come to the conclusion that our efforts during that period have been practically worthless. I see no improvement in preventing forest fires; this destructive practice continues year after year. The past two months of destructive fires have demonstrated the correctness of my statements. There is something radically wrong with a procedure that does not get any better results in a quarter of a century. Farmers do not adopt practices over a generation that do not give them an advantage in some way. They may not understand the basic reasons, but they are thoroughly aware of the results. Let's quit asking [the farmer] not to burn the woods and get down to the basic principle of the matter and give him a substitute that will answer his need and leave him satisfied. He will then not want to burn the woods.

After a favorable report by Nelson and Dutton, on August 3, 1943, Chief Forester Lyle Watts approved control burning for national forest lands in the longleaf and slash pine types. He granted authority to burn for several purposes: protection, seedbed preparation, brown spot disease control, understory vegetative suppression, grazing, and wildlife habitat improvement. He advised Regional Forester Kircher to pass this information on to field personnel, state agencies, and interested private owners. Although burning was approved in August, it was not until December that an informational statement, remembered as the "Treaty of Lake City," was worked out in Florida's Lake City, the headquarters for the Ocala National Forest.

In the meantime another problem was being resolved. It involved the relationship of control burning to a provision of the Clarke-McNary Act of 1922 permitting partial federal reimbursement to the states for fire protection. Kircher announced to the state foresters that the government would henceforth allow federal and state sharing of costs of control burning where the foresters considered it necessary for hazard reduction. After Watts' approval of control burning in the piney woods, meetings on the subject were held with increasing frequency, and control burning proceeded at an accelerated rate. By April 1946, a total of 580,000 acres had been burned in the previous three seasons. By 1982, about 2,800,000 acres of government and private pine lands were burned each season. Some fire management officials have suggested that the control-burn area should be increased to about 8 million acres per season, or about 10 percent of the entire southern pine region.

New Research.   In 1941, I started research on how prescribed burning, timber production, and livestock grazing could be fitted together. This study was a cooperative effort of the Forest Service, Bureau of Animal Industry, and the Georgia Coastal Plains Experiment Station. The Alapaha Experimental Range, a few miles east of Tifton, Georgia, was established and organized for the research.

Since neither total fire protection nor annual burning had proven satisfactory, this new research was organized to evaluate rotational burning. One area was burned every two years and another every three years; a third area was protected and served as a control.

These studies showed that the time and frequency of burning should be geared to the ecological requirements of the trees and the buildup of fire hazards. For longleaf pine, where reproduction is needed, firing can be done prior to a good seed crop and then deferred for one season to allow the seedlings to become established. For slash pine, with a different type of early growth, firing can be done before a good seed crop, and then must be deferred until after the new seedlings are at least five or six feet tall. In this case, native grasses serve as fuels to carry fire in the understory. After these dates, burning can be done as needed to keep the fire hazards down to a reasonable level. These relationships and their practical benefits had been proven in earlier research—and they still hold true.

Control Burning in California

The concept of control burning in California's forests was very controversial in the early days, just as it was in the piney woods. Raymond Clar tells the story well in his book, *California Government and Forestry*, published in 1959 by the California Department of Natural Resources. The Forest Service policy of fire exclusion formulated in 1905 was not finally adopted by the California Department of Forestry until 1924. Between these dates, there was vigorous debate in California about the wisdom of fire exclusion. Two groups emerged. The first advocated light burning in the spring and fall as a means of hazard reduction. Such fires would do about what natural lightning fires and burning by Indians had done for centuries. The theory was that without light burning, the fuels would eventually build up to a point at which a wildfire could not be stopped. Later on, the wildfires would be so intense that nearly all trees, small and large, would be killed over any area burned. Furthermore, the group suggested that light burning might be useful for insect control by keeping down understory competition and removing debris in which some of the insects breed. The second group maintained that wildfires could be stopped without much difficulty and that fire exclusion must be the policy.

Among the strong advocates of light burning were members of the Walker family of the Red River Lumber Company in Shasta County. From 1909 to 1913 the Walkers made a thorough test of light burning on nearly 1 million acres of pine lands under their management. Thirty-five men from Redding were hired to do light burning when conditions were suitable. This group became known as the "needle scratchers." When they could not burn, they piled rocks in the cavities of fire-scarred trees and threw in dirt to keep those trees from catching fire. They also removed logs from near the trunks of trees and used other tactics to lessen the damaging effects of light fires. The cost of burning was, they reported, about 30 cents per acre. This project was given up in 1913 because of outside pressure prompted by the Weeks Act of 1911, which provided for federal and state sharing of the cost of fire control—a provision that the Clark-McNary Act later extended.

In 1919 the controversy over light burning reached a peak when J. A. Kitts of Grass Valley began writing such articles as "Preventing Forest Fires by Burning Litter" and "Prevention of Destructive Forest Fires." Kitts proved experimentally to his own satisfaction the benefits of using fire in the right places at the right time to remove litter. His experimental area was limited to four acres near Grass Valley. Yet, according to Henry Graves, then chief of the Forest Service, Kitts stirred up enough support to undermine public confidence in the Forest Service's fire exclusion policy.

Recognizing this situation, the Society of American Foresters intervened, and the California Forestry Committee was organized to look into the particular problem. Professor Donald Bruce of the University of California was appointed to head the committee. S. B. Show, Forest Service silviculturist, served as spokesman for those against light burning, while Stewart Edward White, a well-known author and a large-scale timberland owner, represented those in favor of light burning.

The committee held three meetings during the winter of 1919–20. On October 14, 1920, it reported to the state Board of Forestry that light burning is a destructive practice founded on false principles of forest protection and conservation. However, the committee's opinion was not unanimous. The lone dissenter was B. A. McAllister of the Southern Pacific Company, who suggested that Kitts' project at Grass Valley be given a fair practical test in the field. McAllister was very concerned about the fire exclusion policy because in July of that year a wildfire along Moffett Creek in Siskiyou County had run through 15 square miles of timberland, doing an estimated $100,000 damage. Much of the burned-over land was owned by Southern Pacific Company. McAllister convinced the committee that the Moffett Creek area would be ideal for field tests of light burning, apparently in the unburned spots skipped by the Moffett Creek fire. Burning tests were carried on here for two full summers in 1921 and 1922.

The committee presented a final report to the Board of Forestry in 1923. It said that the theory of light burning was based on three postulates: (1) that under favorable circumstances, a fire will run through the forest, consuming dead needles and branches, but with little or no damage to living trees; (2) that the intensity of a given fire depends largely on the amount of flammable debris that has accumulated on the ground since the preceding fire; and (3) that complete prevention of fire is not attainable. Opponents of the light-burning theory took the position that (1) even light fires do some damage to mature trees and much damage to young ones; (2) after five or six years, the debris on the forest floor begins to decay at least as fast as it accumulates, and thick tree reproduction is a natural essential to the continuation of the forest; and (3) the USFS had proven by experience that reasonable fire protection was practicable.

The committee reported that the light-burning theory was neither more practical nor more economical than the fire exclusion policy of the Forest Service. Official recognition of this was taken by the state Board of Forestry in August 1924, after which the California Forestry Committee's work was completed. Probably at no other time in the history of forestry has such a major policy as that of fire exclusion been adopted with so little research to support it.

But, as described by Raymond Clar, the ghost of the slain dragon does not rest in peace. After each siege of wildfires, someone questioned the wisdom of the policy of virtual fire exclusion. For instance, after August 1928, without the slightest publicity, Willis Walker of the Red River Lumber Company informed the state forester of the tremendous costs that confronted his company owing to wildfires in his timberlands that season. The company had concluded, said he, that it had best return to the old policy of running light fires throughout its holdings of about 800,000 acres of timber-bearing lands. The deputy state forester, who deplored the idea of light fires, dispatched a letter to Walker in which he proposed that the state and the company cooperate in developing a fire-hazard reduction and suppression plan more in line with modern policies that seemed to hold better promise.

Two young foresters, S. B. Show and his brother-in-law E. I. Kotok, studied the history and role of fire in California forests and jointly published several articles between 1923 and 1930. Both proved to be strong advocates of the fire exclusion policy. Later on, Show became regional forester, a post he held for about 20 years. Kotok soon became director of the Pacific Southwest Forest and Range Experiment Station, where he served for many years. During the administrations of these men, employees of their organizations dared not mention any benefits that might be derived from control burning. It is obvious, then, that these two professionals together had tremendous influence in establishing and securing forest-fire protection policies in California. From 1924 to 1945, there was hardly any use of fire in wildland management, except for piling and burning of logging slash in forested areas.

Burning Permits for Ranchers

In the early forties, many range livestock producers, wildlife groups, and farm advisors observed an increase in brush on livestock ranges and a decline in grazing capacities for both livestock and big game. (To name just two of the most prominent of these observers with whom I worked in Madera County, John O'Neal was a well-known and outspoken cattleman, and Ed Garthwait an energetic and tireless farm advisor.) Futhermore, arson fires were increasing in frequency. Largely as a result of these two problems, the state legislature in 1945 authorized the California Department of Forestry (CDF) to issue burning permits to private landowners who wished to control-burn their brushlands. This policy stimulated a new interest not only in the use of fire (by July 1982, 2,660,000 acres of brushlands had been burned under the permit system) but in other aspects of range management—reseeding, fertilizing, and proper grazing. This period could well be considered the golden age of range management in California, if there ever was one. (See Figure 41.)

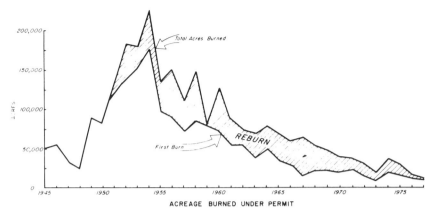

Figure 41. *Acreage burned by California ranchers under permit from 1945 to 1977 to reduce fire hazard and improve grazing for livestock and wildlife. (Graph from the California Department of Forestry.)*

The permit system worked well except for one weakness. It left all the risk and liability for escape fires entirely up to the landowner. The law failed to provide for participation by CDF personnel in the actual burning. If a CDF employee participated and the fire escaped control and caused damage or suppression costs, then that person, and perhaps the CDF, could be sued for wrongdoing. CDF participation was allowed only if a fire escaped rancher control.

The acreage of brushlands burned per year under the permit system peaked in about 1955, when more than 200,000 acres were burned. It then gradually declined because some ranchers had burned twice and had their brush well under control, and more houses were being built in the brushlands, making more critical the danger of fire escapes. But, in addition, some CDF field personnel were continually warning ranchers of the consequences in case of an escape. They went out of their way to explain to ranchers that if a control fire escaped, the foresters would put it out and send them the bill, which ranchers knew could skyrocket within minutes. This admonition was partly a scare tactic. Actually, it did the CDF harm because it made some ranchers distrustful of the organization.

The Objections Continue—
A Personal Account

I worked with ranchers for 13 years, 1947–60, in their burning operations in the foothill woodlands of Madera County. Nearly every Friday afternoon from about July 1 to September 15, I journeyed to the foothills so as to be there early the next morning for a scheduled burn. I learned much from communicating with ranchers and participating in these burns. It was a great experience.

I found that the ranchers were doing an excellent job in planning and carrying out the control burns. They were well organized, well equipped, and proficient in handling the fires. More often than not, 50 to 60 ranchers came to a control burn, which might cover portions of several ranches—up to 2,000 or 3,000 acres.

I got into control burning in California more or less accidentally. When I resigned my research position with the Forest Service in 1947, I went by Washington, D.C., to pay respects to certain foresters there whom I knew. E. I. Kotok, chief of research at that time, said, "Now, when you go to California, don't let them get you involved in research on control burning. Stay out of it and work on grazing problems in the high mountain meadows." I thought this good advice because I knew something about the controversy surrounding fire and figured that I would be continually hampered if I got involved.

However, soon after I arrived in California, Ben Glading, chief of the big-game section of the California Department of Fish and Game, asked if I would be interested in research on the use of fire for big-game range improvement. If so, they could transfer Pittman-Robinson money to the university for this purpose, perhaps in the amount of $25,000 to $30,000 per year. This money was derived from taxes on arms and ammunition; it was not from general taxation. I talked this over with Dean Walter Mulford of the School of Forestry, and he and I then conferred with Dean Claude Hutchison of the College of Agriculture about the proposal. Dean Hutchison considered the research important and suggested that we go ahead with arrangements. Dean Mulford solved the controversial aspect by suggesting that I develop sound research, let the chips fall where they may, and not argue with people but rather listen to them and present facts. I have followed that advice ever since.

Prescribed Burning in Chaparral for Game Range Improvement.   In 1947, our first burning to improve big-game ranges was on Lake County's Cow Mountain, an area of about 65,000 acres. There we learned to do upslope burning in chamise chaparral without installing firelines. This work continued for six years and was · followed by a series of burning experiments on the Lion's Point deer winter range in Madera County.

Understory Burning in Ponderosa Pine.   A bit of information that elevated my endeavors to promote prescribed burning in ponderosa pine was an article in the *Journal of Forestry* in 1943 entitled "Fire as an Ecological Factor in the Ponderosa Pine Region of the Pacific Slope," written by Harold Weaver of the Bureau of Indian Affairs, who worked in Oregon and Washington. He presented a strong argument for the use of fire in the ponderosa pine forests of California, Oregon, Washington, and Montana to reduce fire hazards and discourage forest diseases and insects. Weaver was roundly criticized for his views but continued his observations of the debris-filled, disease- and insect-riddled forests, conditions that he thought were due to fire exclusion. He was clearly ahead of the times and was forced to add a footnote to his future articles, stating: "This article represents the author's views only, and is not to be regarded as an official expression of the attitude of the Indian Service on the subject discussed." He continued using this footnote in his articles for many years, until finally the service became somewhat embarrassed and told him he was vindicated and would no longer be required to add the footnote.

In 1951, I started research at Teaford Forest in Madera County and at Hoberg's Resort in Lake County to evaluate the use of fire in the understory of ponderosa pine. For four years before this, I had been observing and reading about severe wildfires destroying valuable California forests. I reasoned from my experiences in the piney woods of the southeastern United States and from my studies of plant ecology that prescribed fires in

ponderosa pine could reduce fuels to such an extent that summer wildfires would not be so destructive or difficult and expensive to control. I was continually told that broadcast burning could not be done in California because the fuels were either too wet or too dry for burning, and the slopes too steep. The state forester told me in 1950, while we were on a field trip to inspect the results of burning in brushlands, to stay in the brush and grazing lands below and keep out of the forests. They did not want me up there in the pine forests!

Prescribed burning in Teaford Forest and Hoberg's proved easy, highly beneficial, and educational. In early April 1952, I sponsored a field day at Hoberg's to discuss the idea of burning and to demonstrate fire use with a small control burn. (See Figures 42–44.) Some of those present were Paul Sharp, director of the University Agricultural Experiment Station; Fred Baker, dean of the School of Forestry; Ben Madson, chairman of the University Rangeland Utilization Committee at Davis; George Hart, dean of the School of Veterinary Science at Davis; Tracy Storer, chairman of the Department of Zoology at Davis; Henry Vaux, John Zivnuska, and Joseph Kittredge of the School of Forestry at Berkeley; Woodbridge Metcalf of the Forestry Extension at Berkeley; C. C. Buck, in charge of fire research at the Southwest Pacific Forest and Range Experiment Station; and Al Spencer, livestock producer and member of the State Board of Forestry.

Everything went well on the field day except that it was difficult to arouse much discussion or worthwhile comments and suggestions from the group. At least two reasons may have accounted for this: Some were embarrassed by the fact of burning in the understory of ponderosa pine; others did not understand the relationships between fire and other aspects of the environment.

◄——

Figures 42 and 43. *Before (above) and after (below) a prescribed burn at Hoberg's Resort. In starting a prescribed-burning program at Hoberg's, the first step was to reduce the fuels next to the cabins. This was done by raking a fireline alongside the cabins and burning away from them in early morning when cold-air drainage was downslope. After the broadcast burn, the heavy unburned fuels were gradually placed on small fires.*

Figure 44. *The result of a prescribed burn through an area of ponderosa pine. The fire killed 93 percent of 113 living manzanitas without damage to the pines. A second burn killed the remaining manzanita plants and reduced the dead materials.*

Dean Baker did not like the few discussions that did occur after the demonstration burn. About four days after the field day, he wrote me a letter in which he said:

Your field trip to Hoberg's Resort last Saturday was a remarkably fine affair in many ways. It is something that we should get into very much more widely—this gathering of associated interests right out in the field, to see phases of forest land management proposed right on the ground where the chances of misunderstanding are at a minimum. I hope you continue to carry on these demonstrations.

Although I am free to comment most favorably upon the general plan of such meetings and the way in which you handled the discussions, I feel certain that you should exercise the greatest of care in plunging into as uncertain a field as that of the use of fire in forest protection. The reasons are basically two: (1) You know very well the traditional viewpoint of foresters regarding the use of fire in the woods, and I am sure you realize that it is a matter in which many people take a radically different line of thought than foresters. It is easy to misinterpret the objectives and nature of such meetings as the one at Hoberg's Resort, and publicity may readily be spread rather widely over the region where there is a strong tendency towards incendiarism that will make it appear that the School of Forestry is advocating broadcast burning with very little of the necessary restraints and skill in the application of this work. (2) I feel that you should be more conservative in the material which you are presenting and should confine yourself to the use of fire in the improvement of range rather than in safeguarding the forest. The chief reason for this is that you are tackling too big and broad a subject.

In view of this sentiment, I also think it would be very wise of you to withdraw your work from Hoberg's Resort area, since if any group becomes sufficiently opposed to your program to try to undermine it in any way, you are leaving yourself open to very realistic criticism in doing some fine clean-up work for a well-to-do resort owner out of funds that are raised by taxation.

In conclusion, I want you to understand that I am in no way opposed to your work, but I wish that you would be very careful to make it understood that it is your own work, and does not necessarily carry the okay of the School of Forestry as a whole. Also, I would like to have you work carefully to make sure that your points of view are not given too much publicity and are not considered as proven or okayed by any of the forestry agencies, such as the School, the State, or Forest Service here in California.

Dean Baker sent carbon copies of this letter to Dewitt Nelson, state forester; C. C. Buck, one of the participants in the field day; and W. S. Rosecrans, chairman of the State Board of Forestry.

I read this letter three or four times and decided that, unless I could drum up support, I would either have to stop this particular research or be dismissed from the University. I wanted neither alternative, so I rushed to Davis to confer with Ben Madson, chairman of the University Rangeland Utilization Committee. He saw the seriousness of the letter and rushed to Berkeley to see Paul Sharp, director of the University Agricultural Experiment Station, who had attended the field day at Hoberg's. After their meeting, Sharp immediately sent a letter to me praising the work at Hoberg's and expressing the hope that I would be having more such meetings. He sent a copy of his letter to Dean Baker. Baker was then called to Sharp's office and scolded for sending a copy of his letter to Nelson, Buck, and Rosecrans. Sharp said that if there is controversy about one's research and results, it should be kept within the university and worked out there. A few days later, I received the following letter of apology from Dean Baker:

First of all, I do want to apologize for sending my memorandum of April 9 to outsiders, but I had received so much adverse comment from these men, not as individuals, but as channels through which others sent criticisms to me, that I thought it might be a good thing to show them rather definitely that the viewpoints presented at Hoberg's were your own and not necessarily those of the School of Forestry staff as a whole. It was poor judgment to do it that way.

There is no use in our getting too deadly serious on this affair. You are active, a hard worker, and a valuable man. In University organization I am not your boss in the sense the word is commonly used. If I disagree with your views and say so, it is not unlike other differences—they should be limited to you and me personally, however. I freely admit that.

Now don't let my viewpoints bother you too much. The main thing is that you have not persuaded me personally in the correctness of your viewpoints. Exercising academic freedom, I am perfectly free to say that I don't agree with you. As in the past, I shall try to keep my mouth shut as much as possible, but the situation, I think, is such that it would seem wise to proceed with the greatest of care and with full cooperation with your co-workers who are involved in allied problems.

The whole matter seemed serious to the people at Davis. A few days later, Ben Madson, George Hart, and Tracy Storer made a special trip to Berkeley to see Claude Hutchinson, dean of the College of Agriculture. They asked him to promise never to sign dismissal papers for my release from the university. So the upshot was that I continued the research on prescribed burning in the understory of ponderosa pine at both Hoberg's and Teaford Forest until 1965, when I started research on understory burning in mixed-conifer and giant sequoia forests at Whitaker's Forest. Each spring at Hoberg's, I held a field day during which I put on a demonstration burn when weather and fuel conditions were favorable. These field days acquainted many people with the philosophy and concept of prescribed burning, and each year I saw an increase of interest in the work.

Understory burning at Hoberg's and Teaford's was about the only work of this sort in California, since the Walker demonstration was stopped back in 1913. It is inconceivable that such important investigations could be neglected so long. Most investigators wanted to stay away from this activity because it was too controversial. However, I have always reasoned that if there is controversy about something, it indicates a need for investigation and research.

All through the fifties, I was the only person in California doing research on prescribed burning in the understory of trees. My persistence and my refusal to stop the work at Hoberg's led some foresters to view me as being stubborn and headstrong. For example, A. A. Brown, director of Forest Service research in the Washington, D.C., office, wrote to Arthur Hartman of the Southern Region in 1956 that he had

little sympathy with Harold Biswell so far because he has made so little effort to be responsible and constructive. Biswell, I feel, is very headstrong and very much an extremist. He found a pretty strong group of extremists in California when he went there and got a lot of publicity confronting for them.

The extremists Brown referred to were ranchers and sportsmen who were burning under permits from the CDF to remove brush and improve livestock and big-game ranges. All during the fifties, when the ranchers and sportsmen were doing so much burning, professional foresters in general were against it. They could have benefited tremendously by joining in on the burning, but most of them refused. Anyone who did join in with some enthusiasm was likely to be moved to some other position or to some other area far removed from any contact with control burning.

Regarding the comments by Brown, I don't remember that he ever had a discussion with me or attended one of my field days. He apparently was talking from hearsay and imagination.

Some people have wondered how I persisted so long in my research on prescribed burning in the forest understory when there was so much opposition and lack of cooperation. There are several reasons: The burns I undertook in the understory of ponderosa pine were the only research of this sort being done in California; the concept of studying nature and working in harmony with it, not against it, made for interesting work; each year I could see a growing interest in prescribed burning; opposition made it challenging; and many sensible people strongly supported the research and showed it by coming to the field days. On a field day in 1980, at the Calaveras Big Trees State Park, Arthur Jeseau of the CDF, in addressing the group, said: "In the fifties we were all making fun of Harold and fighting him. Now, 30 years later, we are all working for him. This represents quite a change in philosophy and action."

Tall Timbers Research Station.   Tall Timbers Research Station was endowed and organized in large part for studies of the ecology of fire. Since its inception, E. V. Komarek has been its executive secretary. Along with his wife, Betty, these brilliant and energetic people organized 15 conferences of people from all over the world, and as many proceedings were published. There is no better source of information anywhere than these published proceedings. The conferences and proceedings contributed greatly to spurring worldwide interest in the role of fire in wildlands and in the science and art of prescribed burning.

Prescribed Burning at Whitaker's Forest.   Located on a lower slope of Redwood Mountain in Tulare County next to Kings Canyon National Park, Whitaker's is a forest of giant sequoias and mixed conifers. I started prescribed burning there in the understory of giant sequoias in 1965. Shortly thereafter, Richard Hartesveldt, Tom Harvey, Howard Shellhammer, and Ron

———▶

Figures 45 and 46. *Restoration in Whitaker's Forest. After John Muir saw this forest in 1875, he wrote, "In this glorious forest the mill was busy, forming a sore, sad center of destruction." Sugar pine and ponderosa pine were the principal trees cut, but 223 mature giant sequoias—nearly half of the original stand—fell to the axe. The area was later burned and sequoia seedlings appeared in great abundance. The lower picture of a dense stand of sequoias up to 180 feet tall was taken in 1976 after a prescribed burn and some hand reduction of the understory. One wonders what John Muir would say now if he saw this new forest.*

Stecker started studies of burning in giant sequoias on Red-wood Mountain, a short distance above Whitaker's. All these studies showed that the giant sequoia is highly dependent on fire for germination and early survival, so much so that Hartes-veldt remarked that, without fire, the giant sequoia would finally become a rare and endangered species.

In August of each year from 1965 to 1973, when I retired from the university, I conducted a field trip through Whitaker's Forest and put on a demonstration burn over an area that we had burned before. (See Figures 45–46.) The attendance and interest grew each year. On the last field day, 175 attended. I felt that if there had been one more such trip, perhaps 225 to 250 people would have shown up. The demonstration burns in August amazed everyone—elsewhere over the state wildfires were raging.

Burning in National Parks.   In 1962, Stewart Udall, secretary of the U.S. Department of Interior, named a committee to advise on wildlife management in national parks. Headed by A. Starker Leopold of the University of California, the committee saw that pronounced changes had taken place in many parks since 1916 when the fire exclusion policy was adopted. The primitive, open, parklike forests described in the literature had now become filled with debris and understory trees, the animal life had become meager, the wildflowers sparse. To a large extent, the vegetation tangle was depressing, not uplifting. Members of the committee wondered if these forests, with their once abundant wildlife and flowers, could be restored, and, if so, how?

The committee sent in a report in 1963. It suggested that control burning might be the most natural, economic, and feasible way to restore parks to their primitive status. Emphasis was placed on the philosophy and ecological principles involved in national park management. In 1968, fire was reintroduced into the Sequoia–Kings Canyon National Park; fire ecologists Bruce Kilgore and Peter Schuft were prominent in this effort. Shortly thereafter, fire was restored to the ecosystems of Yosemite National Park, the work being directed by Jan van Wagtendonk and Stephen Botti.

The National Park Service's reversal of its official resource management policy of fire exclusion was not recorded in administrative regulations until 1968. According to the new regulations:

The presence or absence of natural fire within a given habitat is recognized as one of the ecological factors contributing to the perpetuation of plants and animals native to that habitat.

Fires in vegetation resulting from natural causes are recognized as natural phenomena and may be allowed to run their course when such burning can be contained within predetermined fire management units and when such burning will contribute to the accomplishment of approved vegetation and/or wildland management objectives.

Prescribed burning to achieve approved vegetation and/or wildlife management objectives may be employed as a substitute for natural fires.

In summary, National Park Service policy now recognizes three types of fires: fires caused by accident; fires set by lightning or other natural causes; and prescribed fires deliberately set to attain a particular management objective. The first type is the people-caused wildfire, and the policy is to suppress it at all times and as quickly as possible. The second is the natural fire, set mostly by lightning, which is allowed to burn if it stays in predetermined boundaries. These fires have been limited to high elevations where vegetation changes have been slow and where the fuel accumulations are not exceedingly heavy. The third type of fire is the prescribed, or control, fire, which is set purposely and is carefully managed back into the ecosystems. Prescribed fires are introduced mainly at lower elevations where fire hazards are extremely critical. Plans for prescribed burning in Yosemite, for instance, require that about 14,000 acres be burned each year in a 13-year burn cycle.

The entire program of fire management in these parks is moving along in excellent fashion, and the National Park Service is to be congratulated for taking the lead in prescribed-fire management activities.

University Extension Courses in Fire Ecology.   In the early seventies, I started teaching two university extension field courses out of the Davis campus: forest fire ecology, in Yosemite National Park and chaparral fire ecology, on Mount Diablo. These proved popular, and later two other courses were added: giant sequoia fire ecology, in the Calaveras Big Trees State Park; and fire ecology basics, in oak woodlands and chaparral of San Diego County. All these were one-unit courses covering two full days, usually Saturday and Sunday. An average of 40 to 45 people attended each course and paid a fee to cover the costs. Emphasizing philosophy and ecological principles, the courses stimulated wide interest in the whole field of fire ecology.

Prescribed Burning in State Parks

Restoration of fire in California's state parks was started in the Calaveras Big Trees State Park in November 1975. The major objective was to carefully reintroduce fire to the various ecosystems so they could operate as naturally as possible—essentially as they would if unimpaired by human activity. (See Figures 47–48.) This philosophy was the same as that involved in the national parks. Glenn Walfoort, state park ranger, lit the match that started the whole burning program, which Fred Meyer, chief of the Natural Heritage Section, had already approved.

By 1982, prescribed burning had been initiated in a half dozen or more of the state parks. The state park system emphasizes training of personnel for prescribed burning, more so than any other state or federal agency. Those heading prescribed-burning projects must have had 12 days of classroom and laboratory training in basic fire ecology, plus 60 days of supervised field experience in burning. All agencies involved in fire ecology would do better work if their personnel took this training.

Control Burning by the California Department of Forestry

In 1980, the governor of California approved Senate Bill 1704, entitled "Prescribed Burning: Brush-Covered Lands." The bill, which initiated a vegetation management program, was enacted in 1981. The law authorizes the CDF to contract with private landowners to control-burn on their properties. It requires

Figures 47 and 48. *Before (above) and after (below) prescribed burning in young giant sequoias. In this case, a prescribed burn was followed by the piling and burning of most of the remaining heavy fuels. Fire danger is now very low.*

that the contracts contain specific provisions relating to equipment, supervision, authority, personnel, insurance, allocation
of costs, and deposits of escrow or trust and disbursal of such
deposits. The law vests in the director of the CDF the final authority to determine the time at which prescribed burning may
be done to minimize the risk of fire escape and to facilitate
maintenance of air quality. It further designates a CDF officer as
the fire boss with final authority to (1) approve and amend the
plan and formula applicable to the prescribed-burning operation; (2) determine that the site has been prepared and that the
crew and equipment are ready to commence the operation; and
(3) supervise the work assignments of CDF personnel, as well
as those of all other personnel hired by the landowner contract-
ing with the CDF, until the prescribed-burning operation is
completed and all fire is declared to be out.

The governor designated about $3 million for this program
for the first year of operation. The plan is to burn 120,000 to
180,000 acres of brush-covered lands per year.

As yet, it is too soon to evaluate the success of this program.
Some ranchers are dissatisfied with the provisions of the law
because they want to do their own burning and not turn it over to
the CDF. All that these ranchers want from the state is standby
service at the time of the fire and liability insurance in case a fire
escapes and damages another property.

Prescribed Burning in National Forests

In 1978, M. Rupert Cutler, assistant secretary of agriculture,
announced a change in policies concerning fire in national forests. Under the revised policy, fire management—prevention,
suppression, and use—will be considered and provided for in
all Forest Service land management plans. Fire management
will be treated as a cost-effective way to meet resource management objectives such as improving wildlife habitat, removing
brush and small trees to improve timber stands, helping prevent the spread of forest insects and diseases, and reducing the
threat of large fires by preventing accumulation of dry forest
debris.

Fire management areas will be established in the national forests, and a set of objectives will be developed for each area through the environmental analysis process with the help of interdisciplinary teams and other agencies and landowners in the area.

Cutler emphasized that, until fire management plans are established, the current national forest fire-protection standard—immediate attack with enough people and equipment to gain control as quickly as possible—will be in effect.

The switch from fire control to fire management in the Forest Service came 73 years after the policy of fire exclusion was adopted in 1905. The principal reason for the change was the growing magnitude of the wildfire problem. It became more obvious all the time that protective burning must be done to reduce wildfire hazards, which was exactly the same reason as that given for the change in fire policy in the piney woods of the southeastern United States in 1943.

An explanation for the persistence of the fire exclusion policy was offered by T. M. Bonnicksen of the University of Wisconsin and R. G. Lee of the University of Washington in their 1979 article "Persistence of a Fire Exclusion Policy in Southern California: A Biosocial Interpretation." They use a systems model to interpret the reason for continuance of the policy. The model links biological, physical, and social elements to adequately map the complexity of the brushland wildfire problem in southern California. The failure to eliminate large and destructive wildfires results in continually increasing losses, which in turn stimulate increasing appropriations of funds for fire exclusion. Greater expenditure, however, does not reduce either value at risk or areas burned, so that losses continue to mount.

And so this chain of events goes on and on with ever more appropriation of funds to exclude wildfires, which in turn assures a buildup of more fuels for more large wildfires and destruction of resources. Prescribed burning should be useful in breaking this chain and minimizing the wildfire problem in southern California.

Chapter Five

Prescribed-Fire Management Planning and Techniques in Burning

Once I was accused of making prescribed burning look too easy. As a matter of fact, it is not difficult. But it does require knowledge of basic fire ecology, careful planning, patience, experience, and know-how. It can be hard work, and there may be cases when surrounding fuels and changes in weather make it nerve-racking.

Selection and Training of Personnel

Not everyone has the temperament and other personal qualities to do prescribed burning. Desirable personal qualities are keen observational ability, good judgment, high power of concentration, high sense of responsibility, and above all, *patience*. Prescribed burners must be interested, alert, and energetic. Burning is not an 8 to 5 job. Occasionally it requires staying out late at night and perhaps on Saturday and Sunday to patrol ongoing fires. However, with good planning and care, such vigilance isn't needed often.

A prescribed burner must have an understanding, gained from field experience, of fire ecology, fire behavior, and techniques in handling fire. It would be difficult for me to name more than a dozen people in all of California who I think have the personal characteristics, ecological understanding, interest, and experience in prescribed burning to be highly qualified for this work. Few people have been selected and trained for this activity. Why? It may be because prescribed burning looks incredibly easy, something that anyone can do by carrying a driptorch and following a textbook prescription. This conception is very wrong!

The best program of training in prescribed burning that I know about is that of the California Department of Parks and Recreation. Its program requires 12 full days of university-caliber training in fire ecology, plus 60 days of field experience in planning and carrying out prescribed burns under supervision. Completion of this training is required of anyone placed in charge of prescribed-fire management programs or who serves as fire boss on burns. (See Figure 49.)

Figure 49. *A field course. An important aspect of prescribed burning is discussing and demonstrating its use and value, as was done here during a university extension course in the fire ecology of ponderosa pine. No one seems to be very disturbed by the smoke: because the size of the fire was controlled, participants could move to the other side of it if their side got too smoky.*

Fire fighters sometimes claim they are qualified to be in charge of prescribed-fire management programs and to carry out prescribed burns. Undoubtedly some are, but most do not have sufficient ecological knowledge or adequate experience in handling prescribed fires. Fire fighters are taught to plan for and suppress wildfires, whereas prescribed burners are selected and trained to set and manage fires for certain objectives and benefits. Experience in prescribed burning gives one an excellent chance to observe fuels and how they burn under varying conditions of weather and topography. It is doubtful that wildfire control activities offer much opportunity for training in prescribed burning: wildfires of low and moderate intensity are too quickly put out to allow observation of fuels and fire behavior and high-intensity wildfires are vastly different from fires used in prescribed burning. When prescribed fires occasionally do escape control, it is often because the burners lack training and experience.

Prescribed-Fire Management Plans

Careful attention must be given to prescribed-fire management planning. The reason is twofold: to assure that all pertinent conditions in an area are studied and evaluated before any burning is done, and to assure that all burns are carried out in orderly fashion and with skill. (See Figure 50.)

Prescribed-fire management plans can take many forms, some more detailed than others. Government agencies often prepare their plans in two steps: a unit plan and a project plan. A unit plan covers an entire unit of management—for example, a state or county park or a ranger district of a national forest. A project plan covers individual burns, or burns in compartments of a unit, to be made during the coming season or year.

Unit plans are more detailed than project plans. They elaborate on the objective in burning; descriptions of the vegetation and other features of the environment, which include fuels, topography, and wind patterns; prescriptions; burning crew needs and responsibilities; constraints; preparations; burning techniques; inspections; record-keeping while burning; patrolling; mop-up; and postfire inspections.

Figure 50. *A landowner being instructed in the art of maintenance burning in his ponderosa pine forest by the author* (right). *This area was first pre-scribe-burned two years earlier.*

Project plans cover essentially the same ground as unit plans but are condensed into a one- or two-page format. Here is an example of such a format.

Condensed Format for Prescribed-Burning
Project Plan (Date: *Nov. 1, 1953*)

Location of burn:	Hoberg's, southwest facing slope below cabins.
Size of burn:	About 20 acres.
Principal objective:	To reduce fuels and fire hazards.
Type of vegetation:	Ponderosa pine/California black oak/nonsprouting manzanita.

Fuel load:	Heavy with dead manzanita and pine needles.
Fuels that carry the fire:	Pine needles spread uniformly.
Topography:	All sloping 20–25%.
Normal wind pattern:	Downslope until about 9:00 A.M., upslope thereafter.
Surrounding fire danger situations:	Cabins immediately above.
Prescription:	Dead fuel moisture 11–12%, air temp. 50°–60° F, humidity 40–45%, soil surface moist.
Date of burn:	Early November.
Burning crew:	Fire boss with two helpers.
Constraints:	Limit rate of fire spread to ¾ ft. per min. and flame height to 1.5–2 ft. over 90% of area.
Preparations:	Obtain fire and air pollution control permits. Notify neighbors of intent to burn. Have fuel-moisture sticks and scales, sling psychrometer, hand wind gauge, notebook, pencil, matches, drip torches and extra fuel, two back pumps with extra water, fire truck (if available), McLeod fire tools, drinking water, first aid kit, safety helmets, and jackets.
Records:	Record dead-fuel moisture content and weather conditions at 2:30 P.M. and describe fire behavior.
Burning technique:	Fire will be set along a raked 4-ft. fireline beside the cabins at 8:00 A.M. when the breeze is downslope. After about 9:00 A.M., the breeze will be upslope and the fire backing downslope.
Mop-up:	Probably not needed.

> *Inspection:*   An inspection will be made soon after the burn to determine coverage of the fire and if objective was attained. The report will record if anything went wrong with the burning and how the operation could have been improved upon.
>
> *Monitoring:*   A yearly inspection will be made until the time of a reburn.

Both unit plans and project plans should be prepared only by people who are knowledgeable and experienced in burning. When the burning is being done, the person who developed the management plan serves as fire boss.

Although ranchers plan their burning with very little paperwork, the planning is done with skill and efficiency. In the central Sierran foothill woodland-savanna where I worked with ranchers for 12 years (1948–60), our procedure was as follows. The county farm advisor and CDF ranger jointly sent a letter to all interested ranchers, inviting them to a planning session. At this meeting, a program was planned for one burn each Saturday during July and August. In some cases, a proposed burn included portions of several properties. For each burn, an inspection committee was named, consisting of three ranchers, the farm advisor, and the CDF ranger. Their objective was to inspect a proposed burn area to determine where the firelines should be and how to prepare them, and to consider other related features. The three ranchers made the decisions, with the farm advisor and CDF ranger acting as consultants. Shortly before the burning, a second inspection was made to see if the firelines were properly prepared, if enough grass remained ungrazed to carry a surface fire, and if all other essentials were in proper order. Ranchers did not hesitate to cancel a proposed burn if they thought preparations were not entirely satisfactory. Later on, one rancher of the inspection team served as fire boss on the burn, with the other two serving as subbosses. Thirty to 60 ranchers usually showed up for a burn, the attitude being "You help me and I help you." (See Figure 51.)

Figure 51. *Ranchers assembled in early morning for a control burn to be started in another hour or so, when the fuels would be somewhat drier. At this burn, 115 people were involved. Equipment consisted of nine water sprayers. Two jeeps were used to patrol the fire.*

The discussion in the remainder of this chapter should be helpful in preparing fire management plans.

Objectives in Burning

The principal objective in burning should be stated in the management plan. It varies with such things as ownership of the land, management policies, the resources, the vegetation, and the soils. Depending on the situation, the main objective may be to reduce fuels and fire hazards, restore fire to its proper role in ecosystem functioning, enhance the wildlife habitat, improve ranges for livestock, reduce understory brush, prepare seedbeds for forest tree planting, stabilize watersheds and improve vegetation-soil-water relationships, or facilitate forest

Figures 52 and 53. *Before* (above) *and after* (below) *three prescribed burns in woodland-savanna. The aim here was removal of brush and digger pine to improve conditions for livestock grazing and for the wildlife habitat and to reduce the wildfire hazard.*

and range management handling practices. Additional objectives might be to improve the health of forest trees, to decrease disease and insect infestations, and to lessen the need for herbicides and insecticides. (See Figures 52–53.)

After reading this long list of objectives, one might conclude that prescribed fires are recommended as a cure for every bad situation. This is not the intention, nor is it the case. Sometimes fire alone is not sufficient and other steps must be taken. For example, close grazing by livestock or heavy browsing by deer can lead to a stand of species of little or no economic value; or cultivation can lead to impoverished soils and, consequently, low-value species. In these cases, grazing and browsing pressures must be corrected either by controlling animal numbers or by improving carrying capacity; the latter might call for prescribed burning, and perhaps also reseeding and fertilizing. Likewise, many undesirable alien plants are adapted to fire and cannot be removed by burning alone—and perhaps not economically by any other means.

Prescribed fires always produce multiple effects. For example, a rancher burns his foothill woodland-savanna to reduce brush and improve grazing, knowing that this burning will also improve the habitat for wildlife, reduce the risk of intense wildfires, increase the flow of spring water, and facilitate handling of livestock. (See Figure 54.)

Prescribed burning in parks and wilderness deserves special comment. The primary objective in most of these entities has been to restore the process of fire to the various ecosystems so they can function somewhat naturally, essentially as they would if unimpaired by human activity. Emphasis is on natural conditions and processes, not on objects. In support of this practice, fire is looked upon as a natural process essential in preserving the integrity, diversity, and stability of the vegetation and other features of the natural environment. Recurring low-intensity fires reduce the fuels and the wildfire hazards, recycle nutrients, rejuvenate plant communities, create scenic landscapes, and maintain natural wildlife habitats. They are also instrumental in thinning overstocked stands of trees and lessening plant diseases and insect infestations. In some high-elevation

Figure 54. *An excellent wildlife habitat in mixed-chamise chaparral, created in part by prescribed burning.*

areas of parks and wilderness, fires set by lightning are permitted to burn themselves out.

Some scientists have suggested that, before reintroducing fire in the forests of parks and wilderness, the saw and axe be used to restore somewhat natural conditions, because some of the larger trees, growing for the past 85 years or so under a policy of fire exclusion, cannot be removed by fire alone. This suggestion is sound ecologically, provided the materials are burned on the plots to recycle nutrients. However, in some cases at least, such an undertaking would be a mammoth task and expensive unless, of course, it were done through a commercial timber operation, a procedure the park and wilderness custodians are not willing to accept at the present time. In some of my own research, broadcast burning was followed by understory tree removal to further reduce fire hazards and to create vistas, colonnades, and openings characteristic of primeval forests. When this procedure was used at Whitaker's Forest, hundreds of incense-cedar up to 35 feet or so in height, but mostly

under 11 feet, were removed to restore more natural and ecologically sound structural stands of giant sequoia with sugar
pine. I recommend this procedure. However, if no cutting is
done, recurring fires will eventually reestablish very natural-
appearing stands. Even one prescribed fire starts visible changes
in that direction.

Descriptions of Areas to Be Burned

Essential items in descriptions of areas to be burned are identification of vegetation types and plant communities, fuel conditions, topographic features, normal wind patterns, size and
shape of areas, and surrounding fire danger situations.

Vegetation Types and Plant Communities

Vegetation types are the major units into which the vegetation
of a region can be divided. They are the product of the environmental factors operative within a region. Philip Munz, in his
California Flora, lists 11 vegetation types. Only six types—coniferous forests, mixed-evergreen forests, woodland-savanna,
chaparral, grasslands, and scrub—are included in this book because they are the ones in which I have done burning and that
are most important from the standpoint of fire occurrence and
use.

Vegetation types are divided into plant communities. These
communities are defined as aggregations of living organisms
having mutual relationships among themselves and with their
environment. Plant communities are identified by naming two,
three, or four indicator species (see Chapter 1, pages 15–17).
For example, in the ponderosa pine community the indicator
species are ponderosa pine/California black oak/manzanita.
Munz lists 29 plant communities, noting the names of the indicator species, the distribution and type of area covered, pertinent climatic data, and the appearance of the vegetation.

Twelve of Munz' 29 plant communities, with a few additions
of my own, such as mixed-conifer forests, giant sequoia, and
eucalyptus, are included in this book. Being able to identify
plant communities is important, because one then better under-

stands how to go about the burning and what can be expected from both fire use and fire exclusion.

The fire management plan should contain a brief statement about the probable occurrence and effects of natural fires in the vegetation and what happens with fire exclusion. This information can be valuable in interpreting the results to be obtained from prescribed burning.

Fuel Conditions

As we saw in Chapter 1, fuels are the organic constituents subject to being burned and include both dead and living materials. For example, in the understory of ponderosa pine, both needles on the ground and small incense-cedars are considered fuels; in chaparral and grasslands, the fuels constitute the total volume of plant material per acre because the entire plant cover is subject to being burned.

Descriptions of fuels are valuable because they give a good idea of how the fires will react, and more important, the probable extent of fire spread over the area to be burned. Elements of a description are the kind of fuels, the amount, size classes, the chemical composition, and the proportion of dead to living materials. The experienced burner can estimate fuel conditions closely enough to judge how the fires will behave and how they should be managed. Usually there is no need to spend days and days measuring volumes of fuels. Remember that only experienced burners should develop prescribed-fire management plans.

Identification of fuels that carry the fires is especially important. The more common ones are conifer needles, dry grasses, oak leaves, chamise chaparral, and coastal sage. The more flammable the fuels, the easier it is to manage prescribed fires, because these fuels will burn when some of the others will hardly ignite. (See Figure 55.)

Topographic Features

Steepness and direction of slope must be described in the fire management plan because they give an idea of how the fires are

Figure 55. *A dense stand of new shrubs that followed a prescribed burn in oak woodland-savanna. This area needs to be reburned to kill the brush seedlings, but there is no fuel to carry a fire. It should have been seeded to annual ryegrass after the prescribed burn to provide fuel for a reburn two years later. Sampling showed 224,769 seedlings of buckbrush and 42,217 of yerba santa per acre.*

going to burn and how they must be set and managed for best results. Contour maps are sufficient to show these two features, but if they are not available, estimates of percentage slope and direction are satisfactory.

Burning on slopes is easier and safer than burning on level ground because slopes offer a degree of fire control. Slopes of 15 to 35 percent are ideal for burning. But slopes are never too steep to be burned, nor is the topography ever too flat. If an area can be burned by wildfires, it can be prescribed-burned, too.

Managing fires on level ground in a forest understory presents the most difficult type of burning. In such places, it is best to burn in small parcels and with a steady breeze. One must proceed with utmost caution and patience, backing the fire against the breeze. A shift in wind direction may cause the flames to go into the treetops. With no wind, the flames go straight up, and since the fire advances slowly, foliage scorching can be excessive.

Nearly all burning in the southeastern piney woods is done on level ground because that is the typical topography. To provide for safety, firelines are plowed in parallel fashion about 200 yards apart to form one-day burning blocks. Fire is then set along all plowed lines simultaneously, so that if the wind changes, the fires burn only a short distance before they come in contact with a burned-over area. Nearly all burning is done against a northwest wind, which usually develops following a storm pattern.

Normal Wind Patterns

As was pointed out in Chapter 1, wind has an important influence on fire behavior. It normally follows certain directions and intensities. For example, in the central Sierran foothill woodlands, the normal pattern is a downslope breeze in the morning until about 9:30 A.M., after which it gradually subsides and starts blowing upslope from the southwest. This wind continues for the remainder of the day, blowing at its greatest intensity between 2 and 4 P.M., the hottest and driest time of the day.

Ranchers in this area who wish to burn with intense fires to kill living brush plan their burning around this normal wind pattern. Fires are set in the early morning on high ground so that they burn downslope with a gentle breeze. Then two crews set fires down both sides of the slope, the fires joining at the bottom at about 2 P.M. Under this plan, most of the burning is done upslope between 2 and 4 P.M., when the wind is strongest, the fuels are driest, and the air temperature is highest. This combination of wind, low fuel moisture, and high temperature gives an intense fire, just what the ranchers want for killing the maximum amount of brush.

In southern California, where Santa Ana winds from the east might cause fire control problems, it is wise to start burning along the western edges of an area and manage the fire so that it burns eastward; then, if a strong east wind suddenly appears, the area in back of the fire will have been burned and the fire itself will be backing against the wind.

Size and Shape of Burn

As a general rule, large units must be broken into compartments that can be burned within a reasonable period and most economically. Several factors combine to determine the size and shape of burns—for example, location of roads and creeks, recent burns, differences in amount and flammability of fuels, and help available to set and patrol the fires.

Preparing firelines can be expensive. Therefore, to keep the costs down, one must plan to make maximum use of roads and trails, creeks, bodies of water, and past burns along which the fires can be set and patrolled.

If the volume of fuels in the understory of trees is moderate to large, one must plan to have the fires move slowly, about ½ to ¾ foot per minute; otherwise foliage scorching can be severe. Obviously, if time is limited, only relatively small areas should be burned. Working in the Calaveras Big Trees State Park, Ranger Glenn Walfoort found that he could burn extremely heavy fuels under very wet conditions. A spot fire was set and nurtured until it was well started. Thereafter, the fuels burned as they were dried by the fire. With the use of this technique, the fires spread only a few feet per hour.

Differences in flammability of fuels must be taken into account. Low-intensity fires in pine needles can be managed so they stop at the edge of a stand of manzanita, where pine needles are absent. Low-intensity fires in grasslands that are dried quickly by sunshine and breezes can be managed so that they stop at the edge of a pine forest, where the fuels are shaded and breezes moderated by the forest stand. Fires in chamise chaparral can be controlled so that they stop at the edge of prior burns made within the past ten years or so. Similarly, fires can be set on south-facing slopes where they will stop at the top of a ridge, where the fuels are less dry. But all this requires experience and expertise in burning.

In addition to these natural features, it may be necessary to prepare firelines. Careful attention should be given to where the firelines are placed. If possible, they should be confined to grass, where the fire can be more easily controlled than in chaparral. A four-foot-wide line through chaparral is not sufficient. Owing to radiant heat, a fire burning in chaparral on one side of a fireline is certain to set fire to the other side. A fireline should be sufficiently free of dry grass, needles, and the like so that a fire cannot creep across it. Finally, all firelines, natural or artificial, should be carefully checked to make sure that no dead branches, if burned off, will fall outside the area to be burned.

Surrounding Fuels and Fire Breaks

Since there is a risk that a prescribed fire might cross a fireline, it is important to study surrounding conditions carefully and note where any escaped fire can be stopped. The more dangerous areas should be indicated on the project plan maps.

Prescriptions for Burning

Prescriptions for burning have two aims: to obtain an effective burn to meet the primary objective, and to manage the fire safely without an escape. Prescriptions relate mainly to the dead-fuel moisture content, air temperature, humidity, wind velocity, soil moisture at the surface, and weather forecasts. Special conditions are sometimes specified. As a safety measure, my prescriptions for first burns in southern California oak woodland-savanna and in chamise chaparral dictate that burning be done only when the surrounding grasses are green and at least two inches tall. In a normal year, this condition prevails from about mid-October to mid-April. Although rain in this area might be sufficient in late August or early September to start growth of grasses and bring them to a height of two inches, it is not wise to start burning that early because the fuels can dry quickly at that season, returning them to high fire-hazard conditions. Furthermore, in southern California, September through November is the period of the most severe Santa Ana winds.

Prescriptions for burning in chamise chaparral and southern coastal sage scrub sometimes include measurements of live-fuel moisture content. In my burning, I have not found it necessary to take detailed measurements. Many observations have shown that these types burn poorly, if at all, when new growth is abundant. The simplest procedure is to schedule the burns outside the period of rapid growth.

The amount of dead material might be more important than live-fuel moisture content. For example, if chamise chaparral has not burned for 45 years and the dead fraction is about 45 percent, the dead fuels might burn with enough heat to dry the living plants to the extent that they burn, too. So, in practice, I look at both the fresh new growth and the dead fraction to decide if satisfactory burning can be done.

Prescriptions for burning vary with the vegetation, the fuels, and the objective. Based on my own research and experiences, the general prescriptions given in Table 3 have proven satisfactory for initial burns. After one or two burns, the dead-fuel moisture content, air temperature, and humidity requirements can be relaxed, and at the same time, the burning can be done more quickly and more safely.

In deciding when to start understory burning, I have learned to rely on fuel-stick moisture content. Not only is the fuel stick easily handled, it is sensitive to changes in weather and is a good indicator of fire behavior and subsequent fire effects. For this reason, I usually check on the fuel-stick moisture content before going into the field to see if it has reached the desirable level specified in the prescription.

Prescriptions for burning can always be improved. One can refine them by taking careful records of each burn after careful observation of the fuels—their characteristics and moisture content and how they burn under the prevailing conditions of weather and other factors influencing the fire—and the results achieved.

Season of Burning

The project plan should indicate with reasonable accuracy the most desirable season for burning both to meet the objective

TABLE 3. Parameters for Prescribed Burning

	Fuel Moisture Content	Air Temperature	Humidity	Wind Velocity	Soil	Weather Forecast
For understory burning in conifer forests and woodland-savanna	fuel stick, 9–12%	35–65° F	30–60%	0 (on slopes) to 10 mph	moist at surface	favorable
For burning in 30-year-old chaparral with the dead fraction about 30%	10-hr. time lag for dead fuel, 12–15%; for live fuel, 75–80%	35–80° F	35–40%	3–5 mph	slightly dry at surface	favorable
For burning in coastal sage scrub and grasslands	10-hr. time lag for dead fuel, 12–15%	35–80° F	35–60%	1–5 mph	slightly dry at surface	favorable
For burning in foothill woodland-savanna to improve conditions for live-stock grazing	10-hr. time lag for dead fuel, 12–15%	85–90° F	30–35%	5–10 mph	dry at surface	favorable
For burning in eucalyptus	fuel stick, 13–18%	35–60° F	35–65%	0 (on slopes) to 10 mph	moist at surface	favorable

and to manage the fire safely. If the primary objective is to reduce heavy fuels in a forested area, perhaps the burning should be done in the fall, after rains but before the fuels become saturated. The advantages of fall burning are that the trees are dormant, cooler days are likely, and the chance of rain is increasing. A disadvantage of fall burning is the chance of a reversal in the weather pattern, bringing back warmer, drier, windy days, when a fire could escape control.

In the understory of conifer forests and in woodland-savanna, where one wishes to limit scorching of foliage to a height of 10 to 12 feet, burning in either the fall or the spring is satisfactory. However, in springtime burning, one must remember the normal weather pattern: cool, moist conditions followed by warmer, drier days. Fires in deep duff are difficult to put out and may continue burning for many days, up to a month or more. This burning can extend well into the summer fire season, creating anxiety among fire control personnel every time a column of smoke is spotted from a tower. For this reason, it is well to stop broadcast burning in deep duff about a month before the normal fire season begins.

Whether burning is done in fall or spring, it is amazing how long fires tend to linger on! I remember a fire set in early May that was still burning 20 feet up on a snag (a standing dead tree) in late August, and a fire set in December that was still burning in May beneath a large sugar pine log that had been covered by snow all winter. Both fires were reducing fuels; and since they were well within the burned-over areas, they were no cause for alarm.

The best season for burning foothill-woodlands to kill brush and improve conditions for livestock grazing is summertime, from about July 1 to August 31. A relatively dry day with a temperature of 85°–90° F is best for this purpose. However, if wildfires elsewhere have the fire suppression agencies occupied, a proposed burn should be delayed for a few days until after fire weather conditions improve. September is usually too dry for burning in heavy fuels.

Number of Days for Burning

Since prescriptions for initial burns in heavy fuels are quite restrictive, one might wonder how many days during a year are suitable for burning. Records for several years of burning in ponderosa pine at Hoberg's Resort show 47 to 74 days good for burning between October 1 and March 31 (see Figure 56). Had the burning continued through April and into May, the number of days would, of course, have been greater. After the fuels in forested areas have been reduced by one or two burns, the

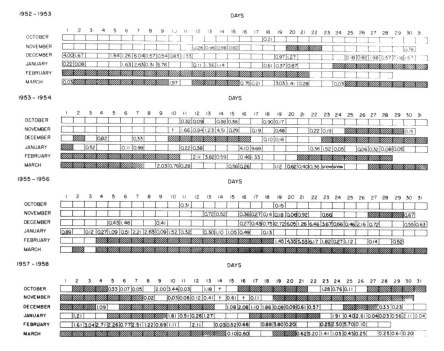

Figure 56. *Days suitable for prescribed burning* (shaded) *in ponderosa pine at Hoberg's from October 1 to March 31 during four seasons. The figures indicate precipitation. The last season is perhaps most typical of what one might expect in this area of high rainfall (approximately 65 inches per year). Because, as this figure clearly shows, each year is different, plans should be made accordingly. In each season, however, there are many days when broadcast burning can be done.*

number of days can be markedly increased by burning earlier in the fall and in late spring and early summer, perhaps to the end of August.

Frequency of Burning

In a given management unit some burning should be done every year to ensure diversity and stability in the vegetation. However, because of the cost, any one compartment (i.e., section of a large unit) should be burned as infrequently as necessary to meet an objective. In a unit of 25,000 acres, perhaps 2,000 to 3,000 acres should be burned per year, with compartments spaced so that the burning will do the greatest amount of good. In a management unit of 300 acres, two compartments of 20–30 acres each year would be sufficient.

In burning to reduce and control understory manzanita in ponderosa pine at Hoberg's, it was necessary to burn four times in ten years to kill the seedlings that came after each of the first three burns. After the fourth burn, only one seedling appeared, and it was browsed by deer. Even 25 years later, there was no need for another burn because the pine needles lay flat on the ground and would not add appreciably to the intensity of a wildfire.

In park and wilderness management, often two or three burns are needed to correct a bad situation. Thereafter, the fires can usually be spaced six to ten years apart. In forests managed for timber, burning should be geared to reducing fuels after each logging.

When prescribed burning is done in woodland-savanna to reduce brush and improve grazing conditions for livestock, a couple of burns, two to three years apart, are very effective in reducing nonsprouting species. The first burn is done to kill shrubs, and the second one to kill seedlings that germinate after the first burn. After the two burns, a well-managed cover of grass is sufficient to keep out brush seedlings.

Constraints on Burning

Constraints placed on prescribed burning can be few or many, depending on such things as policy differences of land management agencies and individuals. As a rule, constraints should be kept to a minimum because they usually add to the cost of burning, and mistakes are common. In certain places, there will be fences and other improvements that must be protected, of course. (The problem of smoke is discussed in the "Clean Air" section of Chapter 6.)

When burning is process-oriented, as in the state and national parks, there need be few, if any, constraints. In this case, management is directed toward *naturalness*—not snags, not deer, not flowers, not open, parklike conditions. The aim is to get fire back into those ecosystems to simulate pristine conditions as closely as possible and to restore a balance of nature.

On the other hand, when burning in parks and wilderness tends to be object-oriented, there can be many constraints: for example, protecting snags for cavity-nesting birds, and building firelines to keep fire out of riparian zones and away from highways (because black looks ugly to some people). Under this policy, human intervention comes into play, and mistakes are frequent because constraints are sometimes imposed without full knowledge or recognition of what the final results will be.

One can always be sure, however, that a constraint imposed for one purpose will have an effect somewhere else in the ecosystem. Snags raked around and saved for cavity-nesting birds will increase fire hazards beyond normal because they are prime targets for lightning strikes and rapid ignition and spread of wildfires. Protecting the vegetation in riparian zones from prescribed fires can lead to a buildup of fuels and perhaps an intense destructive wildfire at some later date. Keeping fire away from highways results in heavy fuels along the roadsides, where people-caused wildfires are frequently started. Building firelines to protect such objects and zones can sometimes lead to soil erosion, can often spoil the appearance of the landscape, and is always costly to management. Generally, it is better to let the low- or moderate-intensity prescribed fires determine which snags will be left for the birds and how the vegetation in riparian zones and along highways will develop naturally, about as it would without human intervention.

People sometimes want to keep prescribed fires out of areas where rare and endangered species are found. But this well-intended constraint can sometimes backfire. One must keep in mind that native plants and animals are best adapted to the environmental conditions under which they evolved. When those conditions are changed, the least adaptable species are the ones most likely to become rare and endangered. So possibly the best way to preserve rare and endangered species is to restore a semblance of their natural environments, the ones in which they evolved. In nearly every case, that means restoring fire to its proper and natural role in the environment.

Interestingly, I do not know of a single case where a plant or animal is rare and endangered because of prescribed burning. On the other hand, I know of several cases where plants considered for rare and endangered status flourished after a prescribed fire. Whitney's sedge in Yosemite Valley was considered for rare and endangered status but became abundant after a prescribed fire. Many other plants, such as fire poppy and whispering bells, are seldom seen in fire-protected areas. However, after a fire they may be seen in abundance because of their dependence on it for seed germination and early survival.

The giant sequoia was considered for endangered status at one time because of its lack of reproduction in some groves. In the 400-acre South Grove of giant sequoias in Calaveras Big Trees State Park, not a single young giant sequoia less than one foot tall could be found in 1975. However, three growing seasons after a prescribed burn in December of 1980, literally thousands of seedlings were growing there and doing well. In this case, fire was essential for seedbed preparation; heat also opened additional cones and released seeds over the burned areas.

It is sometimes difficult not to impose constraints on burning in park and wilderness areas where the objective is to work toward naturalness. The following three cases are examples.

In the South Grove of giant sequoias in the Calaveras Big Trees State Park lie two very large and beautiful sequoia logs that have been there for many years, covered here and there with lichens, mosses, small shrubs, and trees. Prior to setting a prescribed fire in this area, we decided to keep fire away from the two logs by removing the debris that had long been accumulating there. It was either that or see the logs burn. Our defense: The fuels around the logs were unnaturally heavy as a result of many years of fire exclusion. It seemed wise, therefore, to correct the bad fuel situation before the initial burn.

In the second case, in the same grove, we decided to rake the debris from around the giant sequoias, about 1,000 in number, to protect them from fire, because earlier observations had shown that the bark of this species is fibrous, highly flammable, and easily blackened. These precious trees, some of which have been living there 750 to 1,200 years or more, we thought deserved this special treatment. Our defense: Again, the fuels around the trees had become abnormally heavy as a result of many years of fire exclusion, and besides, some people do not like to see blackened trees (see Figure 57). As to whether these objects, logs and trees, will be given special treatment in

Figure 57. *Preparing for a burn. To avoid scorching this giant sequoia, the fuel, which had been accumulating for perhaps 80 years, was moved three or four feet away from the trunk, and the prescribed fire was set on the tree side of the fuel in the evening; thus it burned away from the tree during the cool of the night.*

reburns will have to be determined at some later date. It will probably be best not to apply any special treatment but let the fires burn as nearly naturally as possible.

The third case was in Cuyamaca Rancho State Park in San Diego County. Snags for cavity-nesting birds were scarce because for many years the required practice was to fell the conifers as soon as they showed evidence of beetle infestation and to treat them with an insecticide. As this practice resulted in fewer snags than one would normally expect to see in a park managed for naturalness, we opted to artificially protect some of the snags by raking away the debris. Our defense: A mistake was made earlier and this action was needed as a corrective measure.

Preparations for Burning

Informing and educating people are such important aspects of prescribed burning that they should be started now and continued on a regular basis. People have heard Smokey the Bear's fire prevention message for years and years, but hardly anything on the details of using fire constructively or about the idea of working in harmony with nature. People can be informed through lectures, field trips, newspapers, radio, and television. Demonstrations of setting and managing low- and moderate-intensity fires and showing the immediate results are highly effective.

A marvelous job of informing the local people was done at the Calaveras Big Trees State Park. Through many illustrated lectures and field trips, Ranger Walfoort thoroughly informed the people about the natural role of recurring fires in forests and the facts about intentionally using fire in park management. Fire prevention and fire suppression, he explained, are both essential in park management, but, unfortunately, they allow the fuels to accumulate and the understory forest to become so thick that a wildfire there on a dry, windy day could hardly be stopped. Under present conditions, we stand to lose in a single afternoon of a dry, windy day everything we have been striving so hard to preserve, including the ancient giant sequoias. Also, Walfoort pointed out, the wildlife suffers as a result of the smothering effect of the debris and the understory thickets of trees. The whole area thus becomes a biological slum! Once alerted to these facts, the local people became very supportive of the new prescribed-burning program in the park. Once, after we'd been burning all day and causing considerable smoke in the park's atmosphere, I spoke to a couple of men resting on a fence near headquarters and asked if they had been bothered by the smoke. One replied, "No, this is clean smoke; it's not that Los Angeles stuff."

Before burning, one must get a permit from the proper fire and air pollution control authorities, and then make sure that the public is informed of the burn by newspaper, radio, and television. The media alert becomes less important as a program progresses because the people learn that when they see smoke, it is a prescribed burn. A weather forecast should be obtained shortly before setting the fire; but it should not be relied on 100 percent because, as everyone knows, it can sometimes be wrong. A change in wind direction or velocity is the weather factor to be most concerned about. It is well to proceed in planning and burning as though a change in wind might occur at any time.

One should see that all necessary tools and equipment are on hand and in good working condition. It is embarrassing to have a fire cross a control line and discover that the backpumps are out of order. It is still more embarrassing to learn that not a single person in a crew of nonsmokers brought along a match for ignition. Following is a list of items to have on hand: fuel-moisture sticks and scale, sling psychrometer and tables, wind gauge, notebook, pencils, matches, drip torches, fuel oil (a mixture of 70 percent diesel oil and 30 percent regular gasoline), backpumps and water for refills, fire truck on standby (if available), McLeod fire tools, axes, chain saw, shovels, drinking water, first aid kit, safety helmets and jackets, and hand radios (if available).

There should be enough help to set and manage the fire. A large burn of 1,000 acres or so in woodland-savanna, where the objective is to complete a burn in one day, might require 15 to 20 people. On small burns in ponderosa pine, three or four

people are usually sufficient. Reburning small areas in ponderosa pine, where fuels have been reduced to a low level, can
be done by two or three people.

Each member of a burning crew should be fully acquainted
with the project plan and the area to be burned in all of its aspects. And the responsibility of each person in the burning
operation should be made clear.

Burning Techniques

For successful burning, careful management of the fires themselves is perhaps even more important than the prescriptions.
Several techniques can be employed to govern how fires behave
in different situations of vegetation, objectives, fuels, topography, and weather. The spread of fire is governed by three basic
types of fire: backing fires, head fires, and flanking fires. *Backing fires* are set to burn downslope or on level ground against a

Figure 58. *A prescribed fire on level ground in the understory of Monterey
pine. Fires on level ground must always be set to burn against a steady breeze
to control rate of spread, dissipate heat, and avoid scorching of foliage.*

steady breeze. They can be managed to burn slowly with low flames and low or moderate intensity. *Head fires* are set to burn upslope or on level ground with a wind. They move fast and may become intense in heavy fuels. *Flanking fires* are set to spread at right angles to the slope or to the wind. Their rate of spread and intensity is about intermediate between that of the backing fire and that of the head fire. (See Figures 58-59.)

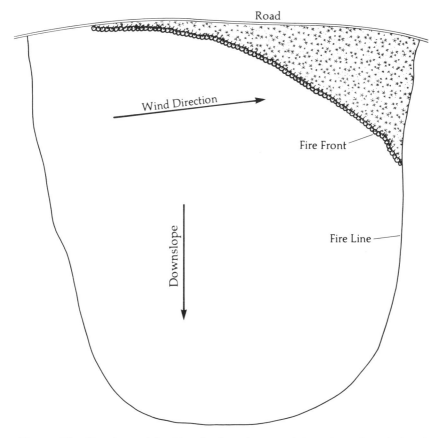

Figure 59. *One form of flanking fire burning at a 45° angle to the wind and to the slope. The fire is set slowly and patiently at the two ends of the fire front and directly ahead of the main body of fire. By this means, the flame is pulled toward the fire and the risk of fire escape is at a minimum. The rate of fire spread is determined by the rate at which the fires are set.*

Backing fires are recommended in heavy fuels, particularly in forests and woodlands where one of the constraints might be to limit foliage scorching to a specified height. Fires are set along the tops of ridges under conditions where they will spread downslope at the rate of ½ to ¾ foot per minute. The edges are secured by setting fires downslope three to four feet ahead of the backing fire. In this way, the flames on the edges are drawn inward by the backing fire, and the danger of fire escape is at a minimum. This technique is especially useful for avoiding fire escapes.

If backing fires move too slowly, they can be boosted to move faster by using strip head fires. These fires are set a short distance downslope below the backing fire and are allowed to burn upslope, coming in contact with the backing fire above. This technique is excellent, but it must be used with caution or the fire will become too intense. One must remember that a fire backing downslope with flames 12 to 18 inches high can easily reach a height of 12 to 15 feet in a distance of only 10 to 12 feet. Beginners in prescribed burning are advised to go slowly in using this technique so that they can develop refined judgment about fire behavior in relation to the fuels and about the distances at which the strip head fires are set downslope. In some cases these fires might be set downslope only a foot or so, whereas in other cases they can be set several feet.

Head fires are very useful for burning in light fuels of forests and woodlands as well as in chaparral and grasslands where there are no trees to be scorched.

Flanking fires are of value in moderately heavy fuels where backing fires may move too slowly and in areas where the fuels have been reduced by one or two previous burns. The technique is excellent as an aid in regulating the rate of fire spread and the fire intensity and in maintaining fire control generally. Flanking fires of the type I use are set and managed so they burn at right angles to the slope or to the wind or both, as illustrated in Figure 59, p. 143. Realizing that there might be confusion about the way I use flanking fires and the way others use them, I checked a glossary of fire terminology and found this definition: "Fire set along a control line parallel to the wind and allowed to spread at right angles to it, toward the main fire." (To me, this definition doesn't make any sense.)

Circular, center, and spot burning are other techniques in setting and managing fires. The first two are not recommended because of the danger of escape. Circular burning involves setting fire completely around the area or a pile of debris to be burned. Center burning involves setting fire in the center of an area and then on the edges, the idea being that the center fire produces inflow of air and pulls the flames inward. Both methods can cause high fire intensity, erratic winds, and strong convection, sometimes strong enough to lift burning materials high into the atmosphere. At this point, many spot fires can cause escapes. A better technique is to set a backing fire on one side of an area or debris pile, under conditions of relatively dry fuels and steady breezes. By this means, the fuel consumption is good, smoke yield is low, and danger of fire escape is at a minimum.

Spot burning consists of setting many spot fires over an area being burned. This technique is widely used in the eucalyptus forests of Australia, where the topography is not steep. The spot fires are set from airplanes under ideal burning conditions. Each fire burns until it comes in contact with another. The method is rapid and results in a pleasing mosaic of different intensity burns. This technique could be used in large, nearly inaccessible areas of chaparral in southern California.

An excellent technique for reducing fuels in strategic areas of forests and woodlands is to follow broadcast burning with hand piling and then burn some of the remaining debris. A few chunks of fuel are thrown together and set afire. As the fuels burn, more are added, a little at a time to always keep the fires small. The piles are placed five to ten feet away from the trunks of trees to prevent scorching. By this method, one energetic person can keep a half dozen piles going at one time and burn 600 to 1,000 pounds of debris per hour (see Figure 60). Even though the piles are kept small, fire intensity can be sufficient to prevent much visible smoke. The technique applies only to areas that have been broadcast-burned, where there is no danger of fires spreading away from the burning piles. Although this technique appears expensive to some people, and it might be momentarily, the results are long-lasting. It makes maintenance burning easier and safer and is an excellent means of putting people to work and teaching conservation. The tech-

Figure 60. *A small pile of debris being burned in an area already burned by a low-intensity broadcast fire. By adding small amounts of debris at one time, a single person can keep a half dozen or more piles burning at one time.*

nique must be applied with care. There is a tendency for three or four people to congregate around one pile and make it too large and too hot. One should avoid making large piles of debris to be burned at some later date.

Three excellent tools available for setting fire in broadcast burning are the driptorch, the helitorch, and the flame thrower. Each has its advantages and disadvantages. The driptorch is cheap and highly suitable for setting fires in flammable fuels on the edges of firelines. With this tool, the fires can be set precisely where they are wanted. For example, in setting fire in pine needles beside a narrow fireline, the fire can be set exactly on the edge, not one or two feet within the fuel bed. This precision eliminates some of the danger of fire crossing the fireline.

The helitorch cannot match the precision of the hand-operated driptorch, but it is an excellent tool for setting fires in large areas of dense, impenetrable chaparral, especially where the burning is done without prepared firelines. In this case, a large driptorch is suspended from a helicopter and operated from controls within the aircraft. Flying over chaparral by helicopter makes the burning easy and rapid.

The flame thrower is an excellent tool for setting fire in the edge of chaparral. The intense flames create enough heat to dry the fuels and get upslope fires going. In some cases, a combination of the three tools can be used to advantage.

Patrolling Prescribed Fires

Careful patrolling of prescribed fires is essential. One should expect that a fire, in some way, might cross a fireline. If it does and is seen soon thereafter, it can be put out without much difficulty. But if the fire is not seen for a while, it can become large and difficult to control. To facilitate patrolling, the fire boss should designate one person of the burning crew to be responsible for this activity.

Fires are sometimes allowed to burn during the night. If the fire boss thinks there is any danger at all of the fire burning out of control, checks should be made two or three times during the night to see that everything is all right.

Recording Burning Conditions

Fuel moisture and weather conditions should be checked at least once each day, about 2:30 P.M., and recorded. Every two hours from 9 A.M. to 6 P.M. is better. A brief description of fire behavior is desirable. These records could prove valuable in case a fire escapes and does damage to someone else's property. These days, when so many people are ready to sue others, it is well to be prepared to show that there was no negligence involved in the prescribed-burning operation. These records are also valuable in explaining fire behavior.

Inspections and Mop-up

After a prescribed burn has been completed, it is wise to inspect the burned area to see if the objectives have been met, to check if anything went wrong, and to consider what could have been done to improve on the project.

Mop-up is sometimes necessary, but the fires should be permitted to burn themselves out if it appears safe to do so. This tactic will make a more beneficial burn and lessen the cost of the project.

Monitoring

Burned areas should be inspected occasionally to more accurately evaluate the results of the project. According to Harold Weaver, in understory burning in ponderosa pine one should not examine a burned area until ten years later, when accelerated growth really begins to show. For, immediately after burning, a forest might look severely damaged to untrained people, but ten years later it could look very good.

Chapter Six

Effects of Prescribed Burning on Resources

If only one purpose were given for prescribed burning, it would be to help protect against wildfires and thus enhance the resources: soils, water, wildlife, wilderness, timber, forage, clean air, and cultural and visual qualities. This chapter discusses how prescribed fires are beneficial in the management of these resources.

Soils

The effects of fire on soils were well presented in a 1979 publication, "Effects of Fire on Soils: A State-of-Knowledge Review" (USDA General Technical Report WO-7). This report was prepared jointly by a group of eight soil scientists, who concluded:

The one finding that emerges from the literature on the effects of fire on soil is that fire intensity and the resulting degree of exposure of mineral soil to heat govern the degree of response of all soil properties investigated.

Land productivity and soil stability are both adversely affected by excessive heat. These vitally important attributes are unaffected or may even be substantially enhanced if the aboveground fuels are burned at sufficiently low intensity so that soil temperature is not greatly increased. Low intensity fire facilitates cycling of some nutrients, may help control plant pathogens, and generally does not increase soil erosion. On the other hand, intense fire volatilizes excessive amounts of nitrogen and other essential nutrients, destroys organic matter, disrupts soil structure, and may induce water repellancy. These effects all combine to subject the soil to excessive erosion and lost productivity potential.

Included here is a point that justifies emphasis: *the intensity of fire* governs whether a fire has good or bad effects on the soil; generally, low- and moderate-intensity fires have good effects, whereas high-intensity fires have bad effects. Low-intensity prescribed fires can be beneficial in two ways: They can be done under fuel and weather conditions that permit burning without excessive heat on the soil, and they can be done often enough to keep the fuels from accumulating to a point where almost any fire produces excessive heat on the soil surface. Thus, any prescribed burning that lowers the risk of an intense wildfire is a step in the right direction.

Two questions are commonly asked about prescribed burning in relation to soils: Does it accelerate soil erosion? Does it deplete the soil of nutrients? The short answer to both questions is, generally, it does not. Prescribed burning with low-intensity fires at intervals of five to seven years in coniferous forests and 20 to 30 years in chaparral will neither accelerate soil erosion over the normal natural amount nor deplete the soil of nutrients.

Accelerated Soil Erosion

Some soil erosion is natural; it has always occurred, and it always will. That's why it is referred to as normal natural erosion, something to be expected. The question is: Does prescribed burning accelerate soil erosion over this normal natural amount?

Research and experience show that low-intensity prescribed fires do not measurably increase soil erosion over the natural amounts in forests, woodland-savannas, and grasslands. After prescribed burning in chaparral, one will often see some slight rill and sheet erosion on slopes. But as William A. McIlride and the watershed management staff of the Soil Conservation Service have pointed out, the advantage of using prescribed fire is that with small portions of the watershed burned over time, erosion and sediment output are moderated over what would occur in a wildfire regime, with large destructive pulses of sediment every 40 years or so. Since prescribed burning decreases the risk and severity of high-intensity wildfires, it helps prevent accelerated soil erosion.

Prescribed fires seldom bare the soil of a protective ground-surface cover. In contrast, a high-intensity wildfire burning in dry and heavy fuels of forest and chaparral under severe fire-weather conditions can remove nearly all the ground-surface cover, thereby exposing bare mineral soil to the pounding force of raindrops. When rain beats on bare soils, small particles are loosened and washed into the macropores, effectively sealing the soil surface against water infiltration. The water can then do nothing but run off, and it might carry soil with it.

In the early days of prescribed burning in the understory of ponderosa pine at Hoberg's, a perennial question posed by skeptics concerned the risk of soil erosion, even though none was seen in areas that were prescribe burned. For this reason, a series of regular-size runoff plots was established on the steepest slope (43 percent) to obtain precise measurements on surface runoff and of soil erosion, if any. Prescribed burning of the plots was done in March, when the soils were damp but the upper pine needles were dry enough to carry a surface fire. About 75 percent of the 10,000 pounds of needles per acre and 25 percent of the 37,200 pounds of duff per acre were burned off. The remaining portions served as a protective ground-surface cover, which was about one-half inch deep and covered 95 percent of the soil surface, as measured by the point-frame analyzer. In addition to this blanket, 1,520 pounds of pine needles, 80 percent of the yearly production in this second-growth forest, fell in late September, October, November, and early December to make the ground-surface cover nearly 100 percent by the time of the first heavy rains in December. During a three-year period, the plots yielded hardly any surface runoff and no soil erosion. The half-inch-deep ground-surface layer of needles and duff protected the soil against raindrop compaction and displacement and maintained high infiltration capacity, sufficient to allow the rainwater, even in heavy storms, to go into subsurface flow and deep seepage.

Within the same general area as the runoff plots were dirt roads, hiking trails, and a skid trail from logging. In these places, the soils were compacted and nearly bare of ground-surface cover, resulting in much surface runoff and evidence of soil erosion. However, as would be expected, the greatest amount of runoff was from a paved road.

Fire can cause the formation of a water-repellent layer beneath the soil surface. This layer increases in depth, thickness, and severity of effect with intensity of fire and is more pronounced in coarse-grained soils like sandy loam than in fine-grained soils like clay loam.

Much of the research on water repellency has been done by Leonard Debano, a USFS soil scientist at Arizona State University in Tempe, who worked in southern California chaparral. He explains water repellency as follows.

Decomposing materials of some plants contain hydrophobic substances that resist wetting. When droplets of water are placed on soil affected by such hydrophobic material, they tend to ball up and remain there for seconds or minutes before being absorbed or running off. Hydrophobic substances are volatilized by fires between soil temperatures of 392° and 550° F. Above the latter figure they are destroyed; and below it some move downward in the soil as gas vapors. When these vapors come in contact with cooler soils (about 482° F), they condense on the soil particles to form a nonwettable layer. At the same time, the soil above is made permeable because the hydrophobic substances there either have been destroyed by heat or have moved downward in the form of vapors. When the soil layer above the nonwettable zone becomes fully saturated with rainwater, it can flow downslope, creating severe erosion problems. The whole situation magnifies with intensity of heat.

Brush and chaparral fuels are sometimes compacted by bulldozers to facilitate safer and more complete burning. This is a poor practice because it increases heat at the soil surface and heightens the water-repellency problem.

Accelerated soil erosion has been observed to be particularly severe following intense wildfires in two situations: first, in southern California chaparral where the slopes are steep and the soils are granitic and unconsolidated; second, in coniferous forests where the fuels were heavy, the soils are friable, and the canopy is destroyed, *leaving no source for the production or deposition of new materials to protect the soil surface.* Furthermore, a fire of uniformly high intensity aggravates the nonwettable condition to a maximum. Under these conditions and with heavy ground equipment in fire fighting, salvage logging, and restoration work, accelerated soil erosion can be severe. Destructive situations of this sort can be avoided if prescribed burning is done to keep the fuels down to a reasonable level where wildfires can be minimized.

Soil Nutrients

Prescribed fires facilitate the cycling of nutrients. Nutrients bound up in debris on the ground surface are concentrated in the ash in forms readily usable by plants. So prescribed burning actually increases productivity.

James Vlamis, of the University of California's Department of Soils and Plant Nutrition, and I tested the effects of burning forest fuels on the availability of nitrogen, phosphorus, and potassium. We took soils from spots where the debris was piled and burned to give "a heavy burn." Pine seedlings growing on the burned-over soils gained nearly 50 percent more weight than those in the unburned areas that served as a check. They responded well to more available nitrogen and phosphorus, but only slightly to the greater amount of potassium, since this soil was already well supplied with this element. In other studies, Vlamis found that after prescribed burning in chaparral, the availability of sulfur increased along with that of nitrogen and phosphorus. (See Figure 61.)

Nitrogen has probably been studied more than any other nutrient in relation to fire because (1) it is deficient in many plant communities; (2) in debris some of it is volatilized by fire in the form of gases; and (3) it is added to the soil by rainfall, dryfall (dry particulate fallout such as windborne dust, pollen, and ash), decomposition, and symbiotic nitrogen fixation.

Debano reported that the amount of nitrogen lost by volatilization depends very much on the intensity of heat: a low-intensity fire will volatilize little nitrogen, whereas a high-

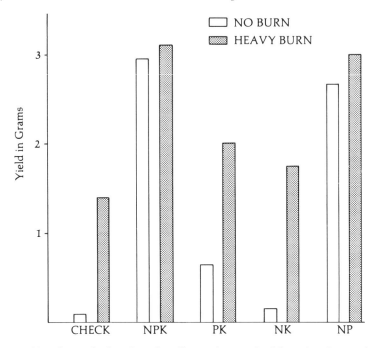

Figure 61. *A graph showing the effects of prescribed burning in ponderosa pine on the nutrient-supplying power of Holland soil from Teaford Forest. Lettuce plants were grown in five 10-inch flowerpots; one received no fertilizer (check); the second was completely fertilized with nitrogen (N), phosphorus (P), and potassium (K); and the others with, respectively, P and K, N and K, and N and P. Burning helped alleviate the deficiency of phosphorus and nitrogen but had no effect on the potassium, which was already sufficient.*

intensity fire can volatilize nearly all of it. Even though part of the total nitrogen is lost as a result of prescribed burning, some is made highly available to plants as ammonia and nitrate-nitrogen, which can stimulate plant growth.

Any nitrogen lost from burning is restored over time. The amount of nitrogen added by precipitation and dryfall is small and variable, depending on the amount of nitrogen in the atmosphere. Nitrogen input from decomposition can be significant after a prescribed burn that does not remove all the nutrient-rich organic layer next to the mineral soil. Greater bacterial fixation occurs after fire because the soil is warmer and sometimes more moist. Leguminous plants such as lupines and clovers and certain shrubs such as ceanothus species and western mountain-mahogany are notable for their nitrogen-fixing bacteria. One study of symbiotic nitrogen fixation indicated that about 600 pounds of nitrogen per acre was fixed by snow brush over a ten-year period. (See Figure 62.)

Prescribed burning can decrease soil acidity, depending on the amount of ash produced, the original acidity of the soil, and the wetness of the climate. Reduced acidity is important because the less acidic condition tends to favor the growth of herbaceous plants as well as to increase bacterial nitrogen fixation. However, understory forest burning with low-intensity fire does not change the acidity much. For example, in pon-

Figure 62. *Volunteer vegetation on a burned area of chamise chaparral in San Diego County. Charred stems of chamise indicate that this area was burned by a moderate-intensity fire. To avoid competition with nonsprouting ceanothus plants, which are valuable in building up nitrogen in the soil, the area was not reseeded to grasses.*

derosa pine at Hoberg's, the acidity was changed from pH 6.0 to pH 7.5 at the soil surface but not at all two inches below the surface. The increased acidity reverted to its prefire level in about two years.

Although prescribed burning in forests reduces debris and other organic materials on the soil surface, it may actually result in an increase of organic matter in the soil itself, because the burning often results in more grasses and legumes. An increase in grasses can be significant because their roots add organic matter directly to the soil itself. Furthermore, the roots are beneficial in maintaining good soil structure, aeration, and percolation capacity.

Prescribed burning facilitates a buildup in soil organic matter in still another way. Small fragments of charcoal are readily washed by rainwater through the unburned portions of the ground-surface cover and into the friable soils beneath. This infiltration could account, in part at least, for reported increases in organic matter in the upper soils of some pine forests burned annually for up to 50 years or more.

Water

Water, an essential wildland resource, can be increased in numerous areas by prescribed burning, whether in oak woodland-savannas, chaparral, or commercial forests. The basic hydrologic principles involved are: (1) reduction of interception losses by removal of fuels; (2) reduction of soil water losses by removal of deep-rooted plants that consume much water in favor of more shallow-rooted species that consume less water (for example, by fire-killing deep-rooted shrubs in oak woodland-savanna to favor shallow-rooted grasses and forbs); (3) reduction of evaporation and transpiration losses in chaparral by growing younger stands through rotational burning; and (4) reduction of interception, evaporation, and transpiration losses in forests through understory broadcast burning and through patch clear-cuttings when harvesting trees. Any increases in water supplies from prescribed burning are hardly worthwhile where the annual precipitation is less than 16 inches.

The greatest increases in water usually come from type conversions, in which all the deep-rooted species are replaced by shallow-rooted ones—for example, the conversion of chaparral or oak woodland-savanna to grass. An excellent report, *Water Salvage Through Vegetation Management in California*, was prepared by Kenneth M. Turner, a watershed management specialist in the California Department of Water Resources. He presents formulas for predicting annual evapotranspiration reductions and gain in salvage water through vegetation management.

Increases in Water Flow

Soon after cattle ranchers in the Sierra Nevada foothills began burning their brushlands, we saw that more water began to flow from some of the springs and creeks. Since these springs are important sources of water for livestock, wildlife, and domestic use, we decided to quantify the amount of water increase from them. The general procedure was to measure spring flow several times before and after prescribed burning. Measurements were made by clocking the time required to fill a quart jar, or by noting the amount of water produced in 15 minutes. The foothills are an excellent area for studies of this sort. Precipitation comes almost entirely in late fall, winter, and early spring, while the summers are long, hot, and dry.

We learned from these measurements that every spring is different. That's because of variations in watershed size, plant species composition, density of brush cover, type of soil, geological formation, amount of precipitation falling on the watersheds, depth of the spring, and source of water. For some springs, it appeared that the water came from outside the local watershed. When spring water is dependent on the local watershed, it is reasonable to expect some increase in flow after a prescribed fire has killed the tops of shrubs and trees and shut off transpiration losses. As we have noted, one of the hydrologic principles involved is the conversion of deep-rooted plants, such as shrubs and trees, to more shallow-rooted species, such as annual grasses and forbs. In this case, some of the moisture left in the soil below the depth of the shallow-rooted species is available for spring flow later in the summer. Furthermore, less precipitation is required the next year to recharge the soil profile, which makes more winter and spring runoff available for flow into storage reservoirs.

In our studies, roots of selected grasses, shrubs, and trees were excavated to get some idea of their depths. Among the annual grasses, soft chess was found to penetrate the soil to a depth of 39 inches, and foxtail fescue to a depth of 23 inches. Both of these annual grasses are important components of the resident vegetation. Roots of three 5-year-old wedgeleaf ceanothus plants were found to extend down more than ten feet, and those of an 11-year-old ponderosa pine were traced down 12 feet, but they went much farther, as indicated by the size of the taproot at the 12-foot depth. Other investigators have found the roots of some shrubs and trees of chaparral vegetation to grow downward more than 25 feet.

Another hydrologic principle involved in spring flow is that some plants have their roots in free water. When the tops of these plants are killed by prescribed fires, spring flow may increase almost immediately. The excavations of wedgeleaf ceanothus gave some indication of how the increase takes place. As we have mentioned, their roots went down 10 feet. Here they came in contact with granitic rocks and were beginning to grow horizontally. At this depth, at the end of April, they were in water flowing over bedrock. Thus, in addition to removing water from the soil, these deeply rooted plants can also tap underground water.

In our studies I saw how prescribed burning increased water flow. Two springs and a creek are discussed below.

Rock Spring.　　The watershed of Rock Spring covers five acres. Annual precipitation is about 24 inches. At the time of the burn the spring water came from a crack down about 10 feet in solid rock. The prescribed fire top-killed about 75 percent of the woody vegetation. Several years earlier, the spring had furnished water all year long for a homesteader. But the present ranch owner reported that in recent years it had gone dry around midsummer.

Before the prescribed burn on July 22, 1950, the spring flow was decreasing rapidly, and the spring finally went dry on July 26. Apparently the water supply had been exhausted by the time of the burn. The watershed was reburned in July 1952. Flow of water was measured several times in late summer in subsequent years, until 1957, when yields varied from 500 to 800 gallons per day.

Tank Spring.   The local watershed is long and narrow and covers about 25 acres. It was burned in August 1950, with a nearly 100 percent top-kill of brush and trees for a considerable distance around the spring. After burning, spring flow increased rapidly for about 15 days until it was more than double that before burning, soaring from a measured 198 gallons per day to 486 gallons.

Finegold Creek.   Two prescribed burns were made in the summer of 1949—the first on July 19, the second on August 20—on both sides of Finegold Creek for approximately one mile. The first burn covered about 4,000 acres, the second about 3,000. The fires top-killed about 10 percent of the riparian vegetation, which consisted chiefly of white alder and mule fat. On the banks and slopes above, the vegetation was typical oak-woodland savanna, of which about 65 percent was top-killed.

Following the July 19 burn, water flow had obviously increased in several places in the creek, but we couldn't determine the amount because no photographs or measurements had been made before the burn. Three days before the second burn of August 20, photographic stations were established in the creek bed, which was nearly dry except for depressions that had filled with water after the first burn. These stations were rephotographed on September 14, about three weeks after the burn, when water in a small stream was flowing down the creek. The appearance of the creek bed before and after the second burn is shown in the accompanying pictures. A word of caution must be expressed regarding photo interpretation here: We cannot be sure how much of the increase in flow might have been due to reduction in transpiration as the days gradually decreased in length. Cooler weather could not have been a

factor since this period was clear, dry, and extremely hot. (See Figures 63–64.)

Prescribed Burning and Water Yield
in Forests

The combination of prescribed burning and timber harvesting in commercial forests recommended later in this chapter can increase water yield in numerous ways. For example, water is increased by (1) reducing debris and small trees in the understory, thus lowering interception loss and permitting more precipitation to reach the soil surface; (2) reducing deep-rooted shrubs in the understory, thereby providing more space for shallow-rooted grasses and forbs that absorb less moisture from the soils; (3) growing younger-age stands of trees where the evapotranspiration loss is less than in more mature forests; (4) maintaining high infiltration capacity so there will be less loss of precipitation through sudden runoff; and (5) maintaining small quantities of leaves and debris on the ground to break the force of raindrops and to ensure high infiltration capacity.

Wildlife

Wildlife includes fauna of all kinds. Nearly every niche of the wildland environment is occupied by some species that has adapted to it. Obviously, if we wish to have wildlife populations rich in number of species, our planning and management must provide for high diversity in habitat conditions. Prescribed burning offers a good technique for doing this.

Wildlife management is looked upon largely as habitat management. Interest and research on the effects of fire have focused

Figures 63 and 64. *Water flow before and after a prescribed burn. The upper picture was taken at Finegold Creek on August 17, 1949, before a prescribed burn on August 20. The lower picture was taken September 14, when the depression had filled with water and flow in the rapids was the size of one's wrist. There was no rain during this period and the temperatures were very high.*

principally on game birds and game animals. However, there has been a growing interest in its effects on small mammals and songbirds. As Jack Lyon and his colleagues put it in their 1978 report on the effects of fire on fauna:

> In general, the larger animals prized as game are reported to increase after fire. For example, moose, white-tailed and mule deer, elk, cougar, coyote, black bear, beaver, hares, turkey, pheasant, bobwhite, sharp-tailed, ruffed, red, and blue grouse, prairie chicken, yellow ptarmigan, heath hen, and some waterfowl have been reported as benefitted by fire. . . . On the other hand, fire may temporarily displace or eliminate species that are dependent on late stages of plant community development such as mountain, woodland and barren-ground caribou, marten, red squirrel, grizzly bear, wolverine, fisher, and spruce grouse. Among the smaller, mostly non-game animal species, the beneficial or detrimental effects of fire are less certain.

This statement refers to wildfires as well as to prescribed fires.

In prescribed burning and managing the habitat for wildlife, it is important to know the characteristics, adaptations, and living requirements of each species. For example, one must know that birds and mammals require year-long food that is palatable and nutritious, and a suitable vegetation cover for loafing and resting, breeding, and escaping from predators (including humans). Some of the small animals, such as mice and salamanders, require that logs and other debris be on the ground. Woodpeckers need dead trees and snags in which to feed and build their nests. Ground-nesting birds should be protected from fire during the nesting season, which might be five to six weeks, from about April 1 to May 15 in southern California, April 15 to May 30 in central California, and May 1 to June 15 in northern California. Some forest birds feed and nest high in tree canopies and benefit from timber harvesting in long rotations that allow the trees to grow taller and more mature.

In burning to favor desirable kinds of vegetation, one must know that some wildlife species are primarily herb-eating grazers, such as elk, bighorn sheep, mountain goat, bison, and rabbits; others are shrub-eating browsers, such as deer, moose, and pronghorn antelope; while still others are intermediate feeders, such as caribou and burros. Since both wildlife and domestic animals sometimes feed over the same areas, it is well to know that cattle belong to the first group, goats to the second, and sheep to the third. But these foraging categories are not absolute, for, to some extent, all grazers browse and all browsers graze. Very often combinations of animals can be used to govern plant composition and to reduce wildfire hazards.

Some species of birds and mammals adapt readily to new situations and are widespread in distribution, while others adapt narrowly and may not thrive or even survive very long under new situations. Excluding fire from fire-dependent types of vegetation may be detrimental to some wildlife; on the other hand, those species favored by later successional stages of vegetation may not be favored if fire is routinely used to manage the vegetation.

Two classic examples—the bobwhite quail and Kirtland's warbler—illustrate the differences in habitat requirements among wildlife species and how fire is used to satisfy their needs.

Bobwhite Quail

A tremendously important upland game bird in the longleaf–slash pine forests of the southeastern United States, the bobwhite quail was rapidly declining in population for some unknown reason when an association of sportsmen requested the U.S. Biological Survey to investigate this phenomenon. Herbert Stoddard, Sr., was sent to investigate the problem. Very soon he found the population decline to be caused by fire exclusion, which allowed the understory ground vegetation to become decadent and to interfere with quail movements and feeding. The leguminous plants, whose foliage and seeds are the quail's primary foods, had declined in abundance. Stoddard suggested control burning as the most natural and economical way of restoring and improving the bobwhite quail habitat. His technique of burning in winter and early spring, when the quail were not nesting, worked so well that it soon became a regular practice in quail habitat management throughout the longleaf–slash pine region. At the same time, other investigators found that control burning improved cattle grazing and was beneficial, if not necessary, in growing longleaf pine timber. But perhaps the greatest benefit from control burning in this area was in reducing fuels and fire hazards, making wildfires easier to control, and at less expense.

Kirtland's Warbler

A rare and endangered small yellow and grey songbird that nests only on Grayling sand among dense young stands of jack pine in northern lower Michigan, Kirtland's warbler is migratory and winters in the Bahamas (see Figure 65). Its song has been

Figure 65. *Male Kirtland's warbler, "bird of fire," at the entrance to its nest. The nest is embedded in the Grayling sandy soil of a dense stand of young Christmas tree–size jack pine that reproduced after a fire. (Courtesy Harold Mayfield.)*

variously described as loud, liquid, wild, and clear. Reports indicate that the warbler will not use just any clump of scrubby jack pine but requires stands of at least 80 acres. This tree is definitely a fire-dependent species with resinous and tightly closed cones. The heat of fire opens the cones for simultaneous seed release and creates ground conditions suitable for germination of the seeds and survival of seedlings. Stands of young jack pine are normally dense and in maximum condition as habitat for warblers at four to 15 years of age or at a height of five to 15 feet. Fire also sets back woody shrubs and brings on a crop of blueberries and grasses that help conceal the nests.

When the forest stand becomes older and the lower limbs die, the warbler moves on to other, more suitable nesting sites, preferably on Grayling sandy soils. For these reasons, the warbler appears to be narrow and specific in its habitat requirements, with Grayling sandy soil seemingly the most important item, and suitable jack pine stands, the second. Historically, lightning and Indian-set fires kept the pine barrens in good shape for Kirtland's warblers. The greatest recent abundance of warblers coincided with lumbering and slash fires around 1880–90. Also, the brown-headed cowbird, a brood parasite of the warbler, had not become a danger at that time. Later, the high success in fire prevention and control in this area threatened the future existence of the warbler. Now that state and national government agencies are logging and burning slash for both timber and wildlife management and controlling cowbirds by trapping in specific nesting sites, we should expect Kirtland's warbler to increase, or at least maintain, its numbers.

The California Condor

The large, wary-type California Condor is another species seemingly not adaptable to change in habitat. There were only 25 to 30 condors in 1980, 20 in 1983, and 5 in 1986, when the remaining birds were trapped for a captive breeding program, in a last-ditch effort to save the species. The last condor in the wilds was captured in April 1987, leaving none to soar in the western skies.

The condor is a scavenger that feeds only on dead flesh. Numerous reasons have been given for its decline, all of which might have played a part: its gobbling up of dead rodents poisoned with 1080 and of carcasses containing lead shot, too much human activity in its territory, too much shooting, collection of specimens for museums, and its vulnerability as a relic of the Pleistocene Age—it might have been declining in number long before Europeans arrived in California.

Raymond B. Cowles, professor of biological sciences at UCLA from 1927 to 1963 and later emeritus professor at UC Santa Barbara, hypothesized that the near-extinction of the condor might be due to fire exclusion from its territory, which has brought about intolerable conditions in its habitat, particularly its food supply. Cowles presented this hypothesis in 1958 in an article entitled "Starving the Condor," and again in 1967 in "Fire Suppression, Faunal Changes, and Condor Diets." As Cowles explained, fire exclusion results in the chaparral growing older, taller, and thicker. In areas of old chaparral, there are only a few rabbits, thought to be the condor's favorite food. Condors were sometimes forced to go long distances for food, mainly the carcasses of domestic livestock, which did not furnish enough calcium for eggshell formation or sufficient nutrition for young birds. Bones of small animals were needed to supply the calcium. Furthermore, in areas of tall chaparral, the condors sometimes had difficulty going into flight when gorged with large quantities of food. They needed running space, just as an airplane needs a runway, to take flight. If condors went into small openings to feed, they got trapped there because of the tall surrounding chaparral. Condors apparently did not feed in the chaparral itself but in ecotones where the chaparral and grasslands meet and where rabbits can be abundant. With fire exclusion, openings in chaparral decreased.

After studying this hypothesis, I wondered how condors could find enough dead rabbits and other foods to satisfy their needs. Even though I knew that rabbits can multiply unbelievably fast with prescribed burning, and I had observed some very large rabbit populations in condor territory, still I wondered about their availability to these scavengers. Under natural conditions, what was it that killed rabbits and other animals on which the condors fed? Or was it natural mortality that made them available? I suspect that the availability of these foods was linked in part to the presence of predators in the natural environment. Prior to the arrival of Europeans in California, large predators in condor territory included the grizzly bear, mountain lion, wolf, and bobcat. Large prey were elk, deer, and antelope—all in addition to the rabbits.

Statements in William H. Brewer's *Up and Down California in 1860–1864* give clues about the probable food supply then found in the general territory of the condor. When camped on the Jolon ranch on the San Antonio River, about midway between San Luis Obispo and Monterey, on May 8, 1861, Brewer wrote:

The American who has this ranch keeps fifteen to sixteen thousand sheep. . . . He says that the loss of sheep from wolves, bears, and rattlesnakes is quite an item. We are in a bear region. Three men have been killed by grizzlies within a year near our last camp.

While speaking of animals—the grizzly bear is much more dreaded than I had any idea of. A wounded grizzly is much more to be feared than even a lion; a tiger is not more ferocious. They will kill and eat sheep, oxen, and horses, are as swift as a horse, of immense strength, quick though clumsy, and very tenacious of life. . . . Less common than bear are the California lions, a sort of panther, about the color of a lion, and size of a small tiger, but with longer body. They are very savage, and I have heard of a number of cases of their killing men. . . . Deer are quite common. Formerly there were many antelope, but they are very rapidly disappearing. We have seen none yet. Rabbits and hares abound; a dozen to fifty we often see in a single day, and during winter ate many of them.

There are many birds of great beauty. One finds the representatives of various lands and climes. Not only the crow, but the raven is found, precisely like the European bird; there are turkey-buzzards, also a large vulture something like the condor—an immense bird. Owls are very plenty, and the cries of several kinds are often heard the same night. Hawks, of various sizes and kinds and very tame, live on the numerous squirrels and gophers.

Brewer moved on to Monterey, and on July 14, 1861, wrote:

Birds scream in the air—gulls, pelicans, birds large and birds small, in flocks like clouds. Seals and sea lions bask on the rocky islands close to the shore; their voices can be heard night and day. Buzzards strive for offal on the beach, crows and ravens "caw" from the trees, while hawks, eagles, owls, vultures, etc. abound. The last are enormous birds, like a condor, and nearly as large. We have seen some that would probably weigh fifty or sixty pounds, and I have frequently picked up their quills over two feet long—one thirty inches—and I have seen them thirty-two inches long. They are called condors by the Americans. A whale was stranded on the beach and tracks of grizzlies were thick about it.

Brewer's party moved on north to Amador Valley, at the south side of Mt. Diablo, and camped on Major Russell's farm. There, on September 12, Brewer wrote:

Game was very abundant—bear in the hills, and deer, antelope, and elk like cattle, in herds. Russell said he has known a party of thirty or forty to *lasso* twenty-eight elk on one Sunday. All are now exterminated, but we find their horns by the hundreds.

Based on Brewer's descriptions, and with a little imagination, one can see that vast changes have taken place in the condor's habitat and territory. It would have been possible to restore the condor's natural environment to some extent through prescribed burning, but even this might not have been enough to halt the decline in condor numbers. If this bird was linked to its natural environment as closely as I think it must have been, the probability of restoring it in the wild is very slim indeed. The changes in its natural environment have simply gone too far.

It seems likely that, rather than trying so vigorously for the past 100 years or so to keep fire out of the condor's territory, fire should have been used all along to simulate some of the naturalness of the condor's territory, the conditions under which it evolved. Of course, prescribed burning would not maintain or restore the animals to which the welfare of the condor was linked, particularly the grizzly bears, for their demise was related directly to the efforts of humans to exterminate them.

Wildlife and Prescribed Burning in Climax Chaparral

Prescribed burning is important in chaparral primarily to reduce wildfire hazards, help stabilize watersheds, and improve the wildlife habitat. Experiments financed by the California Department of Fish and Game were done in North Coast climax chaparral near Clear Lake to improve the game range habitat, particularly that of black-tailed deer. Deer have certain environmental requirements for optimum production—namely, year-long food that is palatable and nutritious, vegetative cover for escape and resting, and drinking water. A shortage or absence of any one of these might make an area unsuitable for deer. With these requirements in mind, we studied the extent to which prescribed burning in climax chaparral affects food availability and consumption, the quality of foods as determined by chemical analysis, and plant succession that can lead to either better or poorer habitat conditions. Responses of deer to prescribed burning included effects on numbers, fawn production, and weight. Other game species studied in less detail included California jackrabbits, brush rabbits, valley quail, and mourning doves.

Prescribed burning was done according to prescriptions given in Chapter 5—that is, burning upslope to create openings of various age classes of chaparral. In a management plan for such burning, about one third of a watershed might be maintained in age classes of ten years or less, one-third in age classes of 11 to 20 years, and the remaining third in age classes of 21 to 30 years. In fact, in this rotation system, no one area would be burned more often than every 30 years, and at the same time, no chaparral would remain unburned for more than 30 years.

Two areas of 1,000 acres each were selected, one to remain in dense mature chaparral, the other to be opened by prescribed burning. Chaparral brushlands in the North Coast region usually consist of two cover conditions—one in which chamise predominates, the other having a mixture of broadleaf shrubs and trees, known as mixed-chaparral. Chamise grows mainly on south-facing slopes and drier sites, while the mixed-chaparral is found on the more moist and cooler north-facing slopes and ravines. This intermixture of conditions is particularly favorable for deer because it provides a wide variety of browse as well as greater seasonal choice. The intermixture in this area, along with available water in ravines, is probably as advantageous for deer as that in any other region of the state. Some climax chaparral lands, particularly those in southern California, are so nearly pure chamise that they furnish relatively poor browse; moreover, in many of those areas, drinking water is in short supply.

Dominant shrubs and trees in the North Coast chaparral are chamise, interior live oak (scrub form), Eastwood manzanita, scrub oak, California laurel, toyon, wedgeleaf ceanothus, deer brush, Stanford manzanita, yerba santa, western mountain-mahogany, and chaparral pea, approximately in that order of abundance. Some of these are more palatable and nutritious than others, and some are hardly browsed at all. The most palatable species are wedgeleaf ceanothus, wavyleaf ceanothus, deer brush, and western mountain-mahogany; the least palatable are the manzanitas and yerba santa; and the other species are intermediate in palatability. Interestingly, all four of the most palatable species are nitrogen fixers, with foliage relatively high in protein content.

A majority of the climax chaparral brushlands in California have shallow soils low in fertility, water-holding capacity, and nutrient-supplying power. Many areas are so steep and rough that, generally, they are suitable neither for tilling nor for conversion to grasslands or forests. Herbaceous vegetation in the understory of climax chaparral is very sparse or nearly absent because of the dense overstory of shrubs and poisonous substances produced by chamise and perhaps some of the other shrubs.

Forage availability was quite different in the burned and unburned areas. In the areas opened by prescribed burning were abundant grasses and forbs. In addition, many of the shrubs were browsed down to such an extent that continual regrowth was easily available to the deer. Edges of unburned patches of dense mature chaparral provided extensive strips along which the deer preferred to browse. Furthermore, the unburned patches of less flammable fuels on the north-facing slopes and in ravines provided an abundance of acorns as well as areas for resting and escape. In the areas of unburned dense mature chaparral, forage was scant. There was hardly any herbaceous forage, and on the north-facing exposures many of the shrubs and trees were tall and out of reach of deer. However, the oak trees did provide acorns. Certain shrubs, such as wavyleaf ceanothus, that normally appear after fire and persist for only a few years were scarce.

Deer are selective in their feeding habits. Usually they take new growth that is high in moisture content, sugars, and proteins; and they like acorns in the fall months. Foods consumed by deer on the two areas—burned and unburned—were determined through stomach analysis, observations, and measurements of shrub use. For the whole year, grasses and forbs comprised 40 percent of the diet in opened chaparral, but only 5 percent in the dense mature chaparral. The grasses and forbs were the preferred foods from January through May—as long as they were green. (See Figure 66.)

The quality of the forage eaten was determined by chemical analyses. For a full year, the protein content of forage similar to that eaten in opened brush averaged 14.4 percent, while that

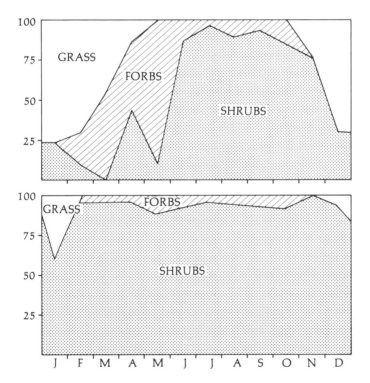

Figure 66. *Graphs illustrating the differences between foods eaten by deer in chaparral opened by prescribed burning* (above) *and those eaten in dense unburned areas* (below). *As can be seen, the big difference is the greater amount of grasses and forbs in the opened chaparral.*

from dense mature chaparral averaged only 9.2 percent. The trend in protein content during the year was similar for both cover conditions, being highest in winter and spring, when herbaceous vegetation was green, and lowest in late summer and autumn before the start of fall rains. The lowest protein content of forage representative of diets in opened brush was 9.2 percent, while in the dense mature brush it was 7.0 percent or less from September through December.

Chaparral brushlands are constantly changing in plant species composition and quality for black-tailed deer and other game species. Some changes take place naturally as the vegetation regrows after burning, some are affected by seasons and time of burning, and others are influenced by different browsing pressures.

As chaparral plants regrow following fire, they gradually become more fibrous and less palatable. After two or three years of regrowth, the understory of herbaceous vegetation begins to decline as the shrubs put out more sprouts and the chaparral thickens. Finally, certain of the shrubs, particularly chamise, produce toxic substances in quantities sufficient to inhibit herbaceous vegetation in the understory; and in some cases, the brush stand becomes so dense that it is nearly impenetrable. However, the situation is not as bad where rotational burning establishes a mosaic of young stands.

Plant succession in chaparral is determined by the frequency and season of burning and by the degree of utilization following burning. Frequency and season of burning are important because some shrubs reproduce after fire from both sprouts and seed, and others only from seed. In addition, the seeds of some shrubs, such as the manzanitas, need more heat than others, such as deer brush, to condition them for germination. Sprout growth usually starts about three weeks after fire, except following winter burns, when the time-lag is longer.

As mentioned earlier, the recommended procedure is to create and maintain a mosaic of young-age stands but not to burn any one area more often than about every 30 years. The main thing is to avoid burning so often that some of the valuable nonsprouting species do not have time to regrow and to produce a new crop of seed before the next burn. If browsing is

Figure 67. *An area burned by a lightning fire 15 years earlier. Heavy brows-ing by deer has prevented seed production. Another fire now would kill the nonsprouting wedgeleaf ceanothus and thus reduce the carrying capacity.*

quite heavy, some of the shrubs may not reach that stage before the age of 15 years, or even longer with close browsing. Burn-ing more frequently, or before the nonsprouting species pro-duce a new crop of seeds, can certainly lead to a decline in that species and perhaps in its carrying capacity. (See Figure 67.)

The season of burning also affects plant species composition. Normally, late summer and early fall burning, when the soils are dry, results in the highest seedling population for all species. Fires in winter—December, January, and February—when the soils are wet, produce fairly good crops of seedlings. However, some of the species, such as manzanitas that require relatively high-intensity heat for germination, may be scarce. After fires in April and early May, the seeds do not normally germinate until the next spring, and by that time the sprouting species have regrown during all the previous year and are well advanced before the new seedlings appear. This situation favors the sprouting species over the nonsprouters, which is not good as far as browse quality of the shrubland as a whole is concerned. Some people suggest that springtime fires over moist soils have a tendency to heat-kill the seeds, but I think the poor germination is due more to passing of the normal rhythmic period of germination for that season.

Since the preferred species are browsed most, they are the ones most likely to decline in abundance. In a mixture of Eastwood manzanita, chamise, and wedgeleaf ceanothus, the last is likely to be browsed so close that it will be killed. Since Eastwood manzanita is not browsed at all, the chamise is browsed more as the wedgeleaf ceanothus becomes scarce, and the manzanita becomes the dominant species. In another case, where chamise grows in association with small quantities of black sage, which is entirely unpalatable, or (as in southern California) with white sage, plant succession tends toward a preponderance of sage. This change in species composition not only results in a decline in carrying capacity but can increase fire hazards since the sages, with their high content of soluble extractives, are extremely flammable. Therefore, a management program should provide for burning rather large areas at one time so that the desirable species are not severely overbrowsed.

Deer population censuses were taken after prescribed burning two times per year, first by the pellet-group count method and later by the sample-area count method. In areas opened by prescribed fires there were 98 deer per square mile in the summer of the first year after burning. The number rose to 131 the second year, and then declined to about 84 the fifth and sixth years. In contrast, counts in the unburned mature chaparral gave a summer density of only 30 deer per square mile.

Fawn production was also affected by the prescribed burns. In opened chaparral there were 145 fawns per 100 does, but in dense unburned chaparral, only 71 fawns.

Deer weight was highest in July. At that time, the deer in opened chaparral were about 13 pounds heavier than those in dense mature chaparral. From that point on, their weight fell. However, bucks in the dense mature chaparral retained their early fall condition better than those in opened brush, probably because they had more acorns. But this situation was short-lived and, from October on, deer weight in unburned areas fell rapidly to a February low of 39 pounds less than the weight of the deer in opened chaparral. In opened chaparral with new grasses and forbs, the bucks maintained their weight well through the remainder of the winter season.

It was evident that in the opened chaparral the generous amounts of herbaceous vegetation, along with the edge effect supplied by the scattered clumps of unburned brush, encouraged the buildup of most resident small game species. The density estimates were based on strip-counts and observations for valley quail, pellet counts for California jackrabbits, and general observations for brush rabbits and mourning doves. In the opened chaparral, valley quail could find abundant herbaceous forage and seeds, with cover nearby. Late-summer populations of 250 per square mile were found in the opened chaparral, but in the dense mature chaparral the number was only 100 per square mile.

California jackrabbits also reached their greatest density in opened brush, where the number fluctuated between 10 and 45 per square mile. The highest counts were made in late summer. In dense mature chaparral, the number was extremely low, only about one per square mile. But brush rabbits were numerous in the dense mature chaparral and in and around islands of such chaparral in the opened brush. Mourning doves were most plentiful in the opened chaparral, with very few in the nearby unburned areas. In opened chaparral, one finds not only the greatest number of deer and most small game species, but cover that is most suitable for hunting. Even species such as the brush rabbit, which are more numerous in heavy than in opened brush, may be hunted more successfully in the latter areas.

In other research in climax chaparral, William Longhurst, professor at UC Davis, also working in the North Coast, found that 55 kinds of birds and 25 kinds of mammals are common to chaparral brushlands. Of this large number only three kinds of birds and two kinds of mammals are sufficiently adapted to extensive stands of mature chaparral to increase their numbers:

namely, Anna's hummingbird, Allen's hummingbird, brown-headed cowbird, Townsend's chipmunk, and dusky-footed woodrat.

Studies by William Wirtz in southern California chaparral reported about the same number and kinds of birds as those found in northern California chaparral.

Prescribed Burning and Wildlife in Foothill Woodland-Savannas. Ranchers in foothill oak woodland-savannas commonly prescribe-burn to reduce brush and improve livestock grazing. The work is done during the summer months in order to kill as much brush as possible. What are the effects of this burning on small mammals and birds that inhabit such areas? Information on the subject was gathered by Professor George Lawrence of Bakersfield College, who studied the vegetation and small mammals and birds for one year before and for three years after a typical prescribed burn on 1,200 acres. His study area was a mosaic of three vegetation communities: oak woodland-grass chaparral, open oak woodland-savanna, and grasslands.

Scientists have concluded that prescribed fires themselves rarely kill any small mammals and birds. The mammals escape these fires either by running away from them or by seeking shelter in burrows beneath the ground surface and in crevices of rock outcrops. However, small mammals can decrease drastically in number within a few days following a prescribed fire because removal of the protective cover exposes them to predators such as coyotes, house cats, red-tailed and sharp-shinned hawks, common ravens, and great horned owls. These predators are highly mobile and can concentrate on burned areas within a short time. Predators are most numerous, of course, on small burns of 50 acres or less. I have seen common ravens flying low behind the flames of grassland fires, apparently searching for small mammals as they become exposed.

Some people have wondered if mammals starve after a prescribed fire. It is doubtful that they do since all seeds and vegetable matter are not destroyed, and unburned spots usually can be found within the boundaries of a prescribed fire. Within a period of two days to three weeks, new food becomes available from sprouting species such as purple needlegrass, poison oak, and shrubs. This new vegetation is highly palatable and nutritious. Populations of small mammals build up rapidly after the start of new growth, and they may shift in species composition from those adapted to oak woodland-chaparral toward those adapted to open oak woodland-savanna or to grasslands. In Lawrence's study, the two small mammals best adapted to open woodland chaparral were the chaparral mouse and the California mouse; the two species best adapted to open oak woodland-savannas and grasslands were the pocket mouse and the field mouse.

Birds, of course, have the unique advantage of being able to fly away from prescribed fires. They have been observed to fly in back of a fire and start feeding almost immediately, apparently on parched seeds and on insects killed by the fire. Bird populations also shift in species composition after a prescribed burn from those adapted to oak woodland-chaparral, such as California valley quail, Bewick's wren, California thrasher, California scrub jay, and brown towhee, to those adapted to open oak woodland-savanna, such as acorn woodpecker, Nuttal's woodpecker, plain titmouse, common bush-tit, western bluebird, house finch, and western chipping sparrow. Or populations may shift toward grassland species such as mourning doves, western kingbird, western meadowlark, and lark sparrow.

Bird populations may also increase as a result of prescribed burning. During the first growing season following a control burn, birds adapted to oak woodland-savanna increased from 347 to 364 breeding pairs per 100 acres, and birds adapted to grasslands from 386 to 441 breeding pairs. These gains were probably aided not only by more foliage and seeds from clovers, filarees, and other forbs that normally increase after burning, but also by more suitable nesting conditions.

Prescribed Burning and Wildlife in Grasslands. Prescribed burning is rarely done in California's 10 million acres of grasslands grazed by livestock. But considerable burning is being done in the grasslands of parks and preserves where the objective is management more in harmony with natural conditions and processes. In these places, the responses of small mammals are about the same as those already discussed for foothill oak woodland-savanna.

Among the birds, one can expect an increase in number the first year after fire, especially of the seed-eating forms, such as mourning dove, western meadowlark, and lark sparrow, owing to more seeds and their greater accessibility. Birds that scratch for their food will be more successful in recently burned areas. In general, the immediate effect of prescribed burning on birds will be to increase their number. As the grass residue accumulates, the bird population would be expected to decline to about what it was before burning.

Prescribed Burning and Wildlife in Forests. The first part of this discussion applies to commercial forests; the second part to forests of parks and wilderness.

If the commercial forest management plan outlined later (see page 188) is followed, deer will probably benefit from the more open, parklike conditions for the following reasons: (1) their diet will be more varied because of the greater amounts of perennial grasses and forbs in the forest understory; (2) their food will be more palatable and higher in crude protein than it would be in dense forests, where there is less sunshine on the lower vegetation; and (3) the forage will be more accessible, and the deer can move about more freely. Deer will find sufficient resting and shading places in the young growth in areas that have previously been clear-cut in small patches. On the negative side, browsing by deer can retard early growth of tree seedlings and perhaps kill some, particularly one-year-old seedlings. Most browsing on seedlings occurs after frosts in the fall when the seedlings are more palatable and at the same time many of the forbs have been killed by the frosts, making the food supply more limited. Browsing damage should not be severe at the higher elevations, where early snows may cover the seedlings and also cause the deer to move off to lower elevations.

Since woodpeckers help control insects in commercial forests, it is wise to have a few dead trees to satisfy their feeding and nesting needs (see Figures 68–69). These can be provided without any appreciable loss to timber growth. If dead trees are too few or absent, it may be wise to girdle a few subdominant

Figure 68. *Debris being removed from the base of a snag before a prescribed burn to save the snag for cavity-nesting birds. Snags were few in this area because of the long practice of felling all snags to reduce the number of lightning fires.*

trees solely for this need. Some forest managers hesitate to leave dead trees that otherwise may produce a small amount of income if sold as fuel wood. Furthermore, they may consider them only as a target of lightning strikes and a source of wildfires.

No studies of bird populations have been made in commercial forests managed as suggested later (see page 188). But such research has been carried out in parks and wilderness. For instance, Bruce Kilgore made a study at Whitaker's Forest, where broadcast burning was followed by piling and burning of debris, which removed 22 tons of dead and down debris per acre plus the debris from cutting on each acre 1,495 incense-cedar and white fir less than 11 feet tall. The altered forest was more open, parklike, fairly free of both debris and understory shrubs and small trees. These are forest conditions that might within a

Figure 69. *Snags for cavity-nesting birds. A few snags are essential for such birds, but this many are not needed and add to the fire hazard. Scenes of this kind are common in fire-protected areas, as the undergrowth develops and creates moisture stress, especially in times of drought. The larger trees are thus made more susceptible to insect attacks. In a program of prescribed burning, where fire prevents the development of undergrowth, this problem is minimized.*

few years be successively control-burned every five to seven years, without any additional piling and burning of debris.

Bird populations were studied both before and after the treatments. Among the birds, two showed a definite increase in number on the burned and manipulated plots: the robin and the western wood pewee. The first is a ground-insect feeder that apparently found more insects on the treated areas. In addition, the treated areas were more suitable for nesting. The western wood pewee is a flycatcher; it typically needs perches on the edges of small openings that command a good view of an untreated area suitable for the detection and capture of its prey. This requirement was met in the burned and manipulated plots.

Four species of birds showed a decrease in numbers after the burning and manipulation treatments: rufous-sided towhee, mountain quail, Nashville warbler, and hermit thrush. Each of these species require brush or dense shady vegetation as part of its habitat. There were few living brush species in the understory, and the removal of small incense-cedar and white fir made an unsuitable habitat for these birds.

The remaining species showed no consistent change in numbers as a result of the manipulation treatments. The most numerous of these species were the Oregon junco, western tanager, and black-headed grosbeak. In summary, as a result of prescribed burning, some birds will increase in numbers and others will decrease in their adjustments to the altered habitat, but overall, the number of birds per 100 acres will remain about the same.

Prescribed burning and forest management have a marked effect on rodents. For example, at Hoberg's we set traps on both treated and untreated ponderosa pine areas. In 1,152 effective trap nights, harvest mice, pinyon mice, and deer mice were caught on the untreated areas, but not a single one on the treated areas. The mice were trapped only on unburned and untreated areas after the trap lines extended into areas of manzanita (both living and dead) and debris. We concluded that the broadcast burning, followed by piling and burning of debris, destroyed the hiding and escape places for these rodents, making them more available to predators—in this case, the great horned owl, since one was often perched in a tree in a treated area.

On several occasions I have been asked about the effects of prescribed fires on yellow jackets. Although definite counts were not made, I have observed that the number of nests is definitely fewer on burned areas than on unburned ones.

Fish Habitat. Fish not only provide food and sport for many people but also are important in the food chain of many animals. The chief benefit of prescribed burning for the fish habitat is the preventive measure of reducing fuels and the damaging effects of wildfires. For instance, the 1987 siege of wildfires in California's national forests damaged nearly 400 miles, or about 20 percent, of the primary fish habitat.

Habitat damage occurs in two forms: (1) in streams, soil erosion sedimentation from severely burned watersheds can cover spawning areas for salmon and trout, and (2) the killing of streamside vegetation allows the water to become slightly warmer and less desirable for cool-water fish. Transport of sediment from severely burned watersheds will last many years, especially where heavy equipment is used in postfire logging operations and watershed restoration.

Wilderness

The Wilderness Act authorizing the establishment of a National Wilderness Preservation System was signed into law by President Lyndon B. Johnson on September 3, 1964. Conservationists had worked many years for wilderness preservation, but it was not until 1951 that Howard Zahniser proposed that wilderness be protected by law. He prepared a bill for Congress in 1955, and it was revised and introduced into the Senate on June 7, 1956, by Senator Hubert Humphrey and into the House four days later by Representative John Saylor. But the bill was too idealistic. So through nine years of deliberation, 65 bills were introduced and 18 hearings held because of controversy mainly over two issues: the areas to be included in the system and the uses that would be permitted in the designated areas. An interesting story of the history of the Wilderness Act is told by Roderick Nash in his article "An Overview—Path to Preservation" in the summer 1984 issue of *Wilderness Magazine.* Nash, a professor of history and environmental studies at the University of California, Santa Barbara, is one of the nation's foremost authorities on wilderness philosophy.

The purpose of the Wilderness Act was to ensure that an increasing population of people would not occupy and modify all areas of the United States and its possessions, leaving no lands in their natural condition for the use and enjoyment of future generations. The act provided that wilderness areas would be carved out of federally owned lands and managed by the department or agency having jurisdiction over them immediately before their inclusion in the National Wilderness Preservation System.

The act recognizes a wilderness area as a place where the earth and its community of life are untrammeled by humans, who are merely visitors—who do not remain. It is further defined as follows: It is an area of undeveloped federal land that retains its primeval character and influence, without permanent improvements of human habitation; it is protected and managed so as to preserve its natural primeval condition, and it generally appears to have been affected primarily by the forces of nature, with the imprint of human work substantially unnoticeable; it has outstanding opportunities for solitude or a primitive and unconfined type of recreation; it has at least 5,000 acres of land or is of sufficient size as to make its preservation and use in an unimproved condition practicable; and it may also contain ecological, geological, and other features of scientific, educational, scenic, or historical value.

Each agency in charge of wilderness areas is responsible for preserving the wilderness character of each area while administering it for such other purposes for which it may have been established. Emphasis in management has been on preserving the physical environment by prohibiting such activities as road building, logging operations, and settlements. Preserving the biological aspects—for instance, retaining the natural character and condition of the vegetation and wildlife populations—has been neglected. The act provides that fire, diseases, and insects may be controlled as deemed necessary by each administrative agency. It must be remembered that these are three of the most important factors influencing the natural character and condition of the vegetation. As a consequence of fire exclusion over the years, vast changes have taken place in the vegetation and wildlife populations. As we've seen again and again, fuels have built up to the point where intense wildfires are doing great damage to nearly all aspects of the environment and are endangering both wildlife and people.

How has fire management in wilderness areas fared since passage of the act in 1964? Policies among federal agencies have varied. The National Park Service (NPS) considers fire as a natural process that should be restored in wilderness areas to keep down the fuels and risk of catastrophic wildfires and to meet the needs of fire-dependent species. The service has many excellent programs for restoring the process through igniting prescribed fires to somewhat simulate those that burned during primeval times. For example, in Yosemite, high-elevation lighting fires are permitted to burn on their own, but they are monitored. A little lower down, where there is more plant growth and fuels, lightning fires are allowed to burn but are monitored and may be suppressed if they are close to a boundary or becoming too intense. Below this zone, in mixed-conifer forests, all wildfires are suppressed and prescribed fires are ignited. Management plans suggest reburning every ten years or so, or more often if time permits. A good plan would be to burn three or four times in close succession to restructure the forest and reduce the fuels so that prescribed burning can be done safely throughout the summer. After this period, prescribed burning could be done as needed to maintain the character and condition of the natural vegetation. Two excellent articles on this are "Fire Management in National Parks" by James Agee in the 1974 summer issue of *Western Wildlands,* and "Restoring Fire in National Park Wilderness" by Bruce Kilgore in the 1975 March issue of *American Forests.*

In contrast to the NPS, the Forest Service did not allow any prescribed fires to be ignited in wilderness areas of California for 22 years after the passage of the act. Being unaware of this policy and noting the fuel and extreme fire hazards in the Agua Tibia Wilderness in southern California, I was shocked to see in the Forest Service's management plan that no prescribed fires were to be ignited within this wilderness. Again, I was amazed to see the same provision in the management plan for the San Rafael Wilderness, also in southern California. Wouldn't it have been better to ignite prescribed fires in such wilderness areas when fire-weather conditions were not severe and when fire-handling techniques could ensure that the fires would be of low to moderate intensity and would reduce the fuel loading and fire hazards without harm to the environment and without danger to the welfare and safety of people? The dreadful Marble Cone Fire that burned about 90,000 acres of the magnificent Ventana Wilderness in 1977—in spite of the efforts of 5,700 fire fighters with the use of 14 air tankers, 15 helicopters, 92 fire engines, and 62 bulldozers at a direct suppression cost of $13 million—should be a lesson to everyone concerned with fire management in wilderness areas.

In 1986 the Forest Service wisely altered its policy concerning fire management in wilderness areas. The new policy permits lightning-caused fires to play, as nearly as possible, their natural ecological role within wilderness and to reduce, to an acceptable level, the risks of wildfire occurring within wilderness or escaping from it. Two types of prescribed fires are now approved for use within wilderness: those ignited by lightning and allowed to burn under prescribed conditions, and those ignited by qualified Forest Service officers.

Essentials in Wilderness Fire Management

The following, I believe, are some essentials in fire management if the purpose of the Wilderness Act is to be attained. These essentials apply not only to federal wilderness but to all parks and preserves regardless of size and management authority.

1. In many wilderness areas that have been under protection for many years and where fuels have become heavy, all lightning fires and other wildfires should be extinguished immediately—not allowed to burn under the prescribed conditions permitted by Forest Service policy. These areas should be control-burned under suitable circumstances. Later, after two or three prescribed fires have allowed the fuels to be reduced to a more natural state, lightning fires can be permitted to burn on their own if under prescribed conditions.

2. Administration must believe that recurring fires are both natural and essential in wilderness and must be willing to restore and use them in management.

3. Administration must be willing to manage for naturalness, not specifically for birds and mammals, nor flowers, but for a semblance of the natural vegetation and environment itself, whatever that might be.

4. Since the purpose of the Wilderness Act is to retain and preserve the character and condition of the vegetation and other conditions of the natural environment, it is desirable to know precisely what these are—for example, the composition

and structure of the vegetation, reproduction patterns, fuel conditions, wildlife populations, and frequency and intensity of free-burning fires set by lightning and perhaps by Indians.

Just as important as learning about these aspects of the natural environment are the effects of suppressing all natural fire on the vegetation, fuels and watersheds, intensity of wildfires, wildlife populations, and other aspects of the natural environment. Information of this sort—the character and conditions of the natural vegetation and other aspects of the environment plus changes brought about by removing one crucial component of the natural environment—can be obtained through studies by fire ecologists applying principles of plant and animal ecology, through observations of fire behavior in prescribed burning, and through records of various kinds such as fire scars on trees, pictures, and descriptions by early-day explorers. Most of this information is already available.

Restoring fire to simulate its natural role in wilderness must be tempered by social, political, and economic constraints. For example, the time and frequency of burning may have to be adjusted somewhat because of smoke concerns in camping sites, or the size of burns may have to be adjusted because of developments adjoining wilderness areas.

5. Administrators must realize that it is hardly feasible to completely restore the natural primeval condition in every case. For example, many of the introduced species, such as slender wild oat, are adapted to and dependent on recurring fires for their general welfare. Fire will not be very effective in removing all of these species. However, in areas where perennial grasses normally grow, prescribed fires can be expected to spur an increase in those species. In some cases it may be necessary to supplement fire with other measures in restoring the natural character and condition; for example, eucalyptus trees may require felling with a chain saw, and heavy fuel loads may be reduced quickly by piling and burning after one or two broadcast burns. All work of this sort must be done carefully and in harmony with the natural ecology of the area.

6. In some cases two or three prescribed fires in close succession and followed by other treatments may be needed to restore a semblance of the natural character and condition of the vegetation.

7. Administrators must use good judgment in management and must depend heavily on that of fire ecologists. Wilderness requires active management, not just management by protection only.

Timber

This section describes how to coordinate prescribed burning and timber management to make both highly effective by better harmonizing with nature. It is my conclusion that yield of wood products can be increased by 50 to 75 percent in those forest types dependent on fire, and probably at one half the cost of present-day management practices where fire is not used and there are big expenses in wildfire control and suppression. Prescribed burning benefits timber production by reducing and modifying fuels to make the forests more fire-resistant and less subject to holocausts, controlling shrubs and understory trees in already well-stocked stands, facilitating logging operations whereby little or no mechanical damage is done to residual trees, and reducing excessive losses from diseases and insects.

We will focus on the ponderosa pine and mixed-conifer types where ponderosa pine is a component of the natural forest stand. As we saw in Chapter 2, this tree is adapted to fire and depends on it for its general good health and optimum growth. The tree is both resistant and adapted to fire, and it produces excellent fuels to carry low-intensity surface fires. Covering some 36 million acres, from the British Columbia Basin in Canada to Durango, Mexico, and from South Dakota and Nebraska to the Pacific Ocean, it is one of our more important timber-producing trees. In California it predominates on around 4 million acres. Unfortunately, the proportion of ponderosa pine in mixed-conifer forests has declined in the past 100 years because of early-day selective logging practices that took the pine, and because of invasions of shade-tolerant species, particularly white fir and incense-cedar, which increase with fire exclusion.

Owing to the nation's need for timber products, I think that the most productive sites should be managed primarily for wood products. These are forests where the dominant trees grow to at least 50 feet in 50 years (site classes IA, I, II, and III). Forests where the dominant trees grow to only 30 or 40 feet in

50 years (site classes IV and V) can very well be managed with more emphasis on secondary resources such as wildlife habitat, livestock grazing, and water yield. One must realize that height growth is normal in moderately stocked stands and is appreciably retarded in both extremely dense and very open stands.

Even though the beautiful primeval forests of these types developed in the presence of recurring surface fires, little research has been done in California on the use of fire to enhance timber production, except for the studies on burning of slash on clear-cut areas and my own research over 33 years.

Suggested Management Practices

The procedures outlined here are based on principles of plant ecology and how these forests developed naturally in the presence of recurring surface fires, and on my own research, experiments, and demonstrations designed to practice timber management and prescribed burning in harmony with nature. The experimental results have been excellent and have convinced me that foresters managing these forest types for timber will someday look upon prescribed fires as their most valuable management tool.

Here is the management plan:

1. Prescribed burning with low- to moderate-intensity surface fires two or three times in close succession to reduce debris and competing shrubs and trees in the understory
2. Patch clear-cuttings of one and a half to three acres at the end of a rotation cycle—either that or shelter-wood harvests of larger size, perhaps five acres each
3. Distribution of the slash as evenly as practical over the ground after patch cuttings; it can then be burned under dry conditions in late August or early September, ahead of a good seed crop
4. Exclusion of fire from these areas until the reproduction is 12 to 15 feet tall and shedding enough needles to carry a gentle surface fire
5. Periodic prescribed burning thereafter through the rotation cycle to eliminate further reproduction and maintain a low fuel level

6. Frequent intermediate harvest cuts
7. Prescribed burning after each intermediate harvest cut to reduce slash fuels and kill brush and tree seedlings.

If sufficient reproduction is not obtained from natural seeding,
planting should be done to bring stocking up to the desired
level. Thus, this plan involves a combination of prescribed
burning, fire protection, select harvesting, and clear-cutting.
(See Figure 70.)

Some forest managers will have difficulty in understanding
why one burns to kill small trees in the understory. In this management plan, one strives to get a crop of tree seedlings, either
natural or planted, after the end of a rotation cycle, and then

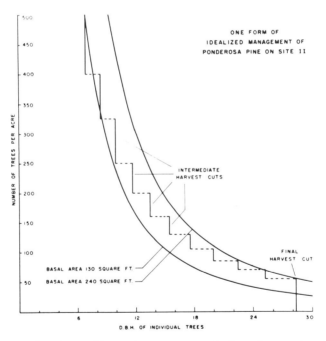

Figure 70. *One form of intensive management of ponderosa pine. With approximately 500 trees per acre at the start, the number removed per acre in
each intermediate harvest cutting is 100, 75, 75, 50, 40, 30, 25, 20, 15, and
15. In the final harvest clear-cut, 55 trees are removed. Since the trees are
growing in open, parklike stands, they can be harvested with little or no damage to the residual trees.*

grows this crop of trees through the next cycle. Any additional seedlings would only slow the growth of crop trees, add to the wildfire hazard, and create droughtlike tree stress favorable to the spread of diseases and insects.

Other managers will think burning slash in August or September ahead of a good seed crop invites fire escapes. However, escapes are avoided by burning in the understory of surrounding trees, perhaps in March or April. Still other forest managers will be concerned about the costs. But I believe it cheaper to follow this plan than to try to manage with poorly stocked stands and mammoth fire hazards and to incur big expenses in fire protection. In addition to these considerations, I believe that environmentalists will be pleased with this approach.

Figure 71. *An experimental plot of ponderosa pines with about 105 trees per acre. Three intermediate thinnings will be made on this plot at ten-year intervals: 20 trees, then 15, then another 15, leaving 55 per acre for a final patch to be clear-cut when the trees are approximately 29 inches DBH (diameter at breast height). Prescribed burning is done after each such harvesting to maintain low fire-hazard conditions.*

Figure 72. *Result of a prescribed burn. This forest was selectively harvested in the fall, and the flammable fuels were reduced by a prescribed burn in March. The wildfire hazard is now reasonably low.*

To understand this management more fully, imagine that we have 3,000 acres, markets are available for timber products, and the objective is to do some harvesting every year. When these forests are properly stocked, the trees grow fast and intermediate harvest cuts can be made frequently, perhaps every ten years on any one area. (See Figures 71–72.)

This management plan suggests a rotation cycle of 150 years. In this case, 20 acres would be the final harvest-cut each year, perhaps in six to ten patches, or fewer if harvested by the shelterwood plan of leaving a few prize trees per acre to produce seeds for the next crop. The first plan of small patch clear-cuts is more in harmony with nature's way of reproducing the forest. Under this system, the forest looks uneven-aged, but in reality it is made up of many even-aged stands or groves, as the accompanying illustration shows.

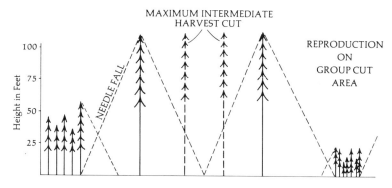

Figure 73. *A sketch showing the pattern of distribution of different age classes, needle fall, and two trees that could be removed in an intermediate harvest cutting.*

This plan facilitates final harvest cuttings in small patches because the open forest permits easy movement of equipment. The minimum size of a patch cut is determined somewhat by the height of the surrounding trees. These trees drop needles into the openings a distance of about two thirds their height. In view of this, the openings must be large enough to prevent the needles from spreading completely across them, otherwise the first prescribed fire might move through the entire opening, thus killing too much of the new reproduction. (See Figure 73.)

In addition to the final harvest cuttings, 200 acres of the 3,000 would be selectively harvested each year in intermediate-harvest cuts. In mixed-conifer forests, the intermediate harvests should be done to favor pine to the extent that about 60 square feet of the basal area of this species remains when the trees are about 10 to 12 inches in diameter. This degree of stocking will allow for the deposit of enough needles on the ground in three years to carry a low-intensity surface fire.

In my research, low-intensity surface fires were used successfully in ponderosa pine–manzanita to kill the nonsprouting shrub and to deplete its seed source stored in the soil and duff. A plot 72 by 72 feet was selectively harvested and prescribed burned in February 1952. One year after burning, we counted 604 manzanita seedlings and 15 ponderosa pine seedlings on the center 60 by 60–foot portion of the plot. The plot was reburned in March 1956 ahead of a good seed crop of ponderosa pine. This reburn killed every seedling on the plot. But one year later, we counted a few manzanita seedlings and 2,159 pine seedlings on the 60 by 60–foot portion of the plot. Another reburn in 1962 killed all the seedlings, both manzanita and pine. Since then the plot has been clear of all seedlings of both species. On the basis of these and other studies I have made, it is obvious that certain harvesting practices and prescribed burning could greatly reduce the need for herbicides to control understory trees and nonsprouting shrubs.

Diseases and Insects

Diseases and insects are a major problem in many commerical forest areas. In many forests more trees die each year from diseases and insects than are havested for timber products. Although pathologists and entomologists have done some excellent research on diseases and insects, little of it has concerned ties to prescribed burning. Yet, with the increasing amount of prescribed burning, no research in forestry is more important than that on the relationship of fire use to diseases and insects. Certainly, large-scale studies should be initiated and involve long-term cooperation among fire ecologists, silviculturists, pathologists, and entomologists.

Perhaps one of the main reasons prescribed burning is effective in controlling diseases and insects is that it thins the trees and reduces understory brush, as outlined in the timber management plan. The result is less competition for soil moisture and thus less stress and less vulnerability to disease. And, as forest managers know, thinning of trees acts as a deterrent to bark beetle attacks, especially during years of drought.

One must also consider whether prescribed burning ever causes disease and outbreaks of insects. In some cases it probably does, especially in areas that have been unburned for many years and where the duff around the trees is deep and contains many feeder roots. After burning in areas of old sugar pine with duff 20 inches deep around the base of the trees, we found that some of the severely scorched trees later showed evidence of beetle attacks. Some of these trees died. Perhaps the fire

Figure 74. *Results of a prescribed burn. An intermediate harvest cut was made in this area, followed by a prescribed burn in November 1956. The young manzanitas that grew after logging were killed in the burn. Young pines in the opening on the right were not damaged by the fire. The photo was taken in June 1958, soon after cattle were moved in for early summer grazing.*

killed the cambium as well as many of the feeder roots and thereby reduced moisture absorption capacity and created too much stress. In addition, this was during a period of severe drought, which probably accentuated the stress factor. If there had been an active program of prescribed burning that occasionally reduced the duff and severity of the fire, the trees might have survived. (See Figure 74.)

Forage

Forage is available in varying amounts in all vegetation types— grasslands, woodland-savannas, forests, chaparral, and scrubs. It includes many species of grasses, sedges, rushes, forbs, and browse from shrubs and trees. These plants vary in their adaptations and responses to fire frequency, season of burning, and fire intensity. And they vary in their habitat requirements, morphology, reproduction strategy, competitive relationships, appeal to different kinds of livestock and wildlife, and responses to different degrees of utilization. Some species are more valuable for grazing than others, some are not utilized at all, and others are poisonous. Familiarity with these features and variables can be useful to fire ecologists in their planning and burning activities.

Recurring fires favor herbaceous plants over woody species and are important in maintaining grasslands. Carl O. Sauer, professor of geography for many years at the University of California, long ago pointed out that all grasslands owe their origin and maintenance to fire. Without recurring fires, all grasslands would eventually be taken over by woody species. (See Figures 75–76.)

Herbaceous plants have a survival advantage over woody species because the perennating buds of perennial herbs and the seeds of both perennial and annual plants are near or beneath the soil surface where they can often escape the killing heat of fire. Furthermore, herbaceous plants, whether annual or perennial, usually grow enough in one season after fire to produce another crop of seed. Postburn growth, along with flowers and fruit-seed production, is often more vigorous than preburn growth. On the other hand, when the tops of shrubs are killed by fire, it takes at least two to five years for them to regrow sufficiently to produce seed, and even longer if they are browsed.

Shrubs vary in their response to fire. In the case of nonsprouting species, two fires, a couple of years apart, are very effective in reducing populations. The first fire kills the shrubs and creates favorable conditions for germination of seed and the survival of seedlings. The second fire kills the seedlings, destroying any future source of seed for further reproduction. However, if there is no second fire within two or three years to kill the seedlings, the result can be a very dense stand of brush. Although populations of nonsprouting shrubs are easily decimated by two fires in close succession, those made up of sprout-

Figure 75. *Two years after prescribed burning in Heise County Park in San Diego County. The ground is covered with wildflowers and grasses. Particularly abundant in this area are true clovers and wild strawberry. This is now an excellent habitat for wildlife.*

ing species are a different matter. If the sprouting shrubs are entirely unpalatable and are not browsed, they are difficult to control with fire; but shrubs that are heavily browsed may be easily killed. One must remember that some shrubs are a valuable source of forage and therefore fire must be used with caution.

Forage on burned areas is generally more palatable, more nutritious, and more available to grazing animals than that on unburned areas. Animals prefer to graze on burned-over acres to such an extent that prescribed burning is sometimes done in out-of-the-way places to bring about better distribution of animals over the range as a whole.

A major problem in range management throughout the western United States has been and still is the encroachment and

Figure 76. *A broadcast-burned area of southern California oak woodland-savanna. After the fire, the remaining heavy fuels were burned as they were piled. A wildfire abetted by Santa Ana winds would now sweep over the ground as a surface fire and do little or no damage to the trees.*

spread of undesirable shrubs and trees over the grasslands and woodland-savannas—species such as oak brush, mesquites, junipers, sagebrushes, buckbrushes, and conifers. These plants not only lower grazing capacities, they interfere with the handling of livestock.

Encroachment of brush began with the introduction of livestock, accompanied by overgrazing and prevention of grassland fires. At first, the encroachment was interpreted to be a response to overgrazing only, and little or no attention was given to the cessation of grassland fires as being a causative factor. It must be realized that, in the early days of settlement, fire was looked upon as strictly a destructive agent, a menace to be prevented at all times. In some quarters, heavy grazing was advocated and encouraged as a means of reducing wildfire hazards. Furthermore, many professionals believed a watershed cover of shrubs and trees to be superior to grasses in preventing water runoff and soil erosion. These ideas were questioned by Aldo Leopold in his article "Grass, Brush, Timber, and Fire in Southern Arizona," published in the 1924 issue of the *Journal of Forestry*.

The country of which Leopold wrote consists of the rough foothills of Arizona, corresponding in elevation to the California woodland type. Above this zone are the forests of ponderosa pine, and below are the desert ranges characteristic of the southern Arizona plains. The area, therefore, is large, comprising the greater part of the Prescott, Tonto, and Coronado national forests, as well as much rangeland outside them. The brush that has "taken the country" comprises dozens of species, in which various oaks, manzanitas, mountain-mahogany, and ceanothus predominate.

Leopold theorized that the combination of overgrazing and cessation of grassland fires accounted for the brush encroachment. Overgrazing weakened the perennial grasses, thereby reducing root competition to the shrubs, with the result that the shrubs and trees grew more vigorously and produced more seed. At the same time, the overgrazing reduced fuels to a point where grassland fires would not spread, or if they did, the fires would be so light they would not decimate the woody species. Leopold's theory was never challenged, and it still holds today. In more recent times, studies of increase of shrubs and trees in areas protected against both grazing and fire have verified what Leopold found and convinced me that the lack of fire was probably more important in allowing the shrubs to increase than was the overgrazing.

Along with brush encroachment, Leopold saw another problem, that of active soil erosion, which was looked upon as more serious than the loss of grazing capacity. Prior to settlement, the lightning fires and those set by Indians had maintained a grassland that was effective in preventing soil erosion, even though the fires were frequent. With accelerated erosion, reservoirs built for the storage of valuable irrigation water soon filled with soil, causing loss of storage capacity or expensive removal of silt.

Leopold also noted that the radical encroachment of brush

in the Arizona foothills had led to some interesting effects on game:

> There is one mountain range on the Tonto where the brush has become so thick as to almost prohibit travel, and where a thrifty stock of black bear have established themselves.
>
> The old hunters assure me that there were no black bears in these mountains when the country was first settled. It is likewise a significant fact that the wild turkey has been exterminated throughout most of the Arizona brushfields, whereas it has merely been decimated further north. It seems possible that turkeys require a certain proportion of open space in order to thrive. Plenty of open spaces originally existed, but the recent encroachment of brush has abolished them, and thus possibly made the birds fall an easier prey to predatory animals.

If recurring fires were effective in presettlement days in maintaining grasses of the Arizona foothills, why can't prescribed burning be done now to restore them to their former status? As a matter of fact, fire is being used in Arizona and other regions of the western United States, mainly to reduce or manipulate brush, but in some areas, the brush has grown tall and largely out of reach of fire and has so completely taken over the landscape that hardly enough grass will grow to carry fires intense enough to have any detrimental effects on the brush. When alternatives or supplements to fire are used, such as bulldozing and chaining, costs become nearly prohibitive.

The following idea might seem radical to some people, but since in certain areas of the southwest the ecological balance between grasses, fire, and soils was so fragile and sensitive in presettlement days, perhaps livestock should never have been introduced into those areas. Conceivably, it would have been better to leave the grasses for their watershed values and for wildlife, using frequent fires to keep out the brush and maintain the grasslands.

Prescribed Burning to Enhance Forage Production

About 85 percent of the wildland forage in California comes from 10 million acres of grasslands and 7.5 million acres of woodland-savanna. These lands are used primarily for livestock grazing, and rightly so. They are very important to the range livestock industry. The other 15 percent of the livestock forage comes from sagebrush-grass, forests, and brushlands. Only the grasslands and woodland-savanna are discussed in this section.

The grasslands are mainly in the dry foothills and plains surrounding the interior valleys extending toward the coast into southern California, and in the central and northern coastal regions. The woodland-savannas are found at elevations above the grasslands and extending into southern California. Representative forage plants in both types are annuals of grasses, forbs and legumes, such as wild oat, slender wild oat, soft chess, ripgut brome, foxtail barley, filarees, popcorn flower, and native clovers. Annuals often account for 98 percent of the plant cover, with introductions from Europe and elsewhere composing 65 percent. Except in the cooler and more moist central and northern coastal regions, only traces of perennial grasses are found, such as purple stipa, pine bluegrass, California melic, and June grass. In the central and northern coastal regions, perennial grasses can be quite abundant, species such as oat grass, tufted hair grass, creeping wild rye, spike bent grass, velvet grass, California brome, and Idaho fescue. Because of the preponderance of annual plants, the grasslands and woodland-savannas together are usually referred to as the annual plant forage type.

Plant ecologists generally believe that perennial grasses were once more abundant and declined because of overgrazing by livestock. I agree, but surely the prevention of frequent fires in postsettlement days also had something to do with the decline. Some of the conclusions about pristine grasslands derived from observations by plant ecologist Frederic Clements. He saw that, along fenced railroads, the "relict" vegetation was largely perennial grasses, particularly purple stipa. Apparently he overlooked the fact, that in addition to being ungrazed, the railroad rights-of-way were control-burned every year to prevent summer wildfires and that that might have contributed to the abundance of purple stipa. In another instance, after the 1923 Berkeley fire, nearly all vacant lots in the hill areas were burned every year to reduce fire hazards. As a result, some of the lots grew nearly pure stands of purple stipa. In the fifties, I took students there each year to show them an example of what pristine grasslands, ungrazed by livestock but burned frequently, might have looked like. Later on, in about 1960, the practice of yearly burning was stopped and changes began to show in the plant cover. Ripgut brome and coyote brush increased, and by 1984, no purple stipa could be found. The yearly fires evidently functioned to maintain purple stipa on the lots in the same way as they had done along the railroad rights-of-way that had been protected from grazing but control-burned every year.

Under a burning regime, purple stipa has several advantages over annual plants: It starts fall growth with very little precipitation and does not suffer as much as the annuals from a lack of grass residue; its summer dormancy seems to be broken by fall fires; and it requires a minimum of about 0.24 inch of precipitation and a few cloudy days to start fall growth, whereas the annuals need 0.85 to one inch. Residue in the amount of 500 to 1000 pounds per acre is very beneficial to annuals in that it helps retain surface moisture and moderates low temperatures. Lesser amounts of residue on burned areas are not critical for the welfare of purple stipa as it is somewhat drought-resistant and, once established, is not so sensitive to cold or drought.

Experience has shown that on ranges where annual plants are managed for livestock grazing, perennial grasses are at a disadvantage as competitors because they stay green longer than the annuals and, being more palatable over a longer time, may be grazed to near extinction even when plenty of dry annual forage is available and the range, as a whole, is moderately utilized. (See Figure 77.)

Only minor shifts in species composition can be expected in the crops of forage annuals as a result of prescribed burning. Wild oat and slender wild oat plants usually grow larger and appear more abundant after burning, probably because they make appreciable late winter and early spring growth and benefit from the warmer soils beneath the black ash, as well as from more available nitrogen. Filarees and native clover are other species that increase after prescribed fires. The seeds of filarees lie beneath the soil surface, where they are protected from fire;

Figure 77. *Prescribed burning on a strip of ungrazed annual grassland at Folsom Lake. The burn was done not only to reduce the wildfire hazard, but also to determine whether perennial species would increase as a result.*

and the "hard" seeds of native annual clovers are conditioned by fire for better germination. These shifts in species composition can be beneficial to livestock and game since both relish the foliage. Also, the seeds of wild oat are a favorite food of wild turkey, and those of native annual clovers are chosen by quail. However, the benefits of such minor shifts in species composition alone would not justify the expense of prescribed burning.

In some parks and preserves ungrazed by livestock but managed for naturalness, prescribed burning may be justified as a means of restoring perennial grasses. Early findings by the California Department of Parks and Recreation and by the Nature Conservancy indicate that the number of perennials in an area can be increased by burning. Two other reasons for burning may be to reduce mats of ungrazed residue that tend to smother the herbaceous vegetation, lowering its soil water-using capacity and making conditions more favorable for shrubs and half-shrubs, such as coyote brush and poison oak; and to reduce damage to the vegetation should a wildfire occur when the mats of residue are dry and under severe fire-weather conditions. Tests showed that heavy mats of residue can be burned when moist at the base without any damage to the underlying vegetation. An example is deer grass, a coarse, relatively unpalatable, densely tufted perennial. When the tops of severely smothered plants were burned with a sweeping surface fire, many new close-tufted shoots and flower stalks sprang up, showing that the plants were greatly stimulated by the prescribed fire. Those smothered tufts would probably have been killed by a summer wildfire.

Prescribed burning in woodland-savannas is another matter. Because brush encroaches over most of such vegetation and presents a severe problem on about 45 percent of it, a great deal of prescribed burning is done as a brush control measure. The degree of success depends strongly on the encroaching species and the burning and management procedures. In the central Sierra Nevada foothills, where I worked with ranchers for 12 years, the principal shrubs to be reduced in the lower portions of the type were buckbrush, chaparral whitethorn, and Mariposa manzanita, all nonsprouting species. At the higher elevations, mainly between 2,500 and 3,000 feet, sprouting shrubs were abundant, such as scrub interior live oak, leather bush, buckthorn, and western mountain-mahogany. In addition to the shrubs, digger pine was considered an undesirable tree that ought to be controlled. This tree produces a gum drip that spoils the forage beneath; and when its needles are on the ground, they interfere with grazing. Ranchers say it poisons their soil, meaning, no doubt, that the soil becomes more acid and produces less forage. In fact, these trees were considered enough of a pest in Madera County to justify a government conservation payment of ten cents per tree to either fell them with chain saws or poison them with 2,4-D.

By contrast, blue oak was a desirable tree throughout the woodland-savanna, worthy of being protected from fire for its aesthetic enrichment of the landscape, shade, wildlife values,

Figure 78. *A prescribed fire in oak woodland-savanna. The fire was set at about 1 P.M. on July 23, 1953, to burn upslope and kill brush plants and digger pine for livestock range improvement.*

and soil-building properties. In some cases, heavy fuels beneath or close to these trees were gently moved away with a small bulldozer prior to prescribed burning. The protection measures were effective: very few mature blue oaks were killed, as indicated by a rancher who said to me in 1985 that he thought not over a half-dozen mature oaks were killed in all of the prescribed burning that had been done in Madera County. (See Figure 78.)

Here is how prescribed burning was done in the woodland-savanna foothills of Madera County. A first burn was made to kill brush and digger pine. Two or three years later a reburn was done to kill the brush seedlings that came after the first fire. Very often, a third burn was made six or seven years after the second one to remove the debris of dead brush, particularly that of digger pine. Any dense brush areas that had been heavily burned by the first fire, as indicated by the presence of white ash, were seeded to annual ryegrass before the start of fall growth in order to have fuel for the second burn. Annual ryegrass was selected for seeding because the seeds are always available at relatively low cost, they are easily applied with a hand seeder, germination and early growth are excellent, and the forage is well liked by livestock and deer. This grass is not a persistent species and after two or three years gives way to resident annuals. Annual ryegrass is a heavy user of soil moisture and nutrients and is very competitive. We found that roots of buckbrush seedlings growing without annual ryegrass competition penetrated the soil to a depth of 40 inches or so by mid-June, and most of them lived. In contrast, the roots of brush seedlings growing with ryegrass competition penetrated the soil only 11 inches or so and died because the soil moisture had been depleted by the ryegrass as it matured.

The combination of treatments we used gave excellent and long-lasting results. In April 1985, I had the pleasure of examining some of the areas that were prescribe burned 35 years earlier and found them in fine condition. I estimated they would be good for another 35 years or even longer without any further burning.

Buckbrush is such an excellent deer browse species that in some cases only one burn, followed by seeding the white ash areas to ryegrass to thin the brush, may be preferable to the two or three burns in close succession.

Since the objective of burning on livestock ranges in woodland-savanna is to reduce brush and digger pine and make more space available for forage, firing is purposely done under dry, hot conditions, as indicated by the prescription in Chapter 5. But in spite of this intention, the fires are not uniform in coverage and spots frequently remain unburned. Occasionally a rancher would use a bulldozer to mash the brush in those areas, so the fuels would be consumed in the second and third burns. An important consideration in prescribed burning is to have enough dry grass fuels to carry the fire from one clump of brush to the next, with sufficient heat to ignite or kill the brush. For this reason, it is often necessary to defer or lighten grazing before burning takes place to ensure sufficient dry fuels to carry the fire.

Results of prescribed burning at the higher elevations and in other places where sprouting shrubs are abundant have not been as dramatic as those where most of the shrubs are non-sprouters. However, because of the recent increase in demand for fuel wood, some of these brush and live oak woodlands have appreciated in value for this commodity, so that getting rid of some of this type of brush by burning is no longer as important as it was earlier.

When woodland-savanna rangelands are burned to improve livestock grazing, there will be other associated benefits: for example, wildfire hazards are reduced, spring flow is improved, and habitat conditions for wildlife are generally better.

Any person wishing to read further on the ecology and use of fire in rangelands forage production will have no trouble in finding many references. Some excellent publications are listed in the suggested readings for the chapter (see especially the works by Daubenmire; Nichols, Adams, and Menke; Vogl; and Wright and Bailey).

Clean Air

Smoke in the atmosphere from forest and wildland fires is a natural phenomenon—just as natural as the fires from lightning and the fog that hides the mountain peaks and causes closure of airports. This smoke is composed of small gas-borne particles, or, more specifically, aerosols, resulting from incomplete combustion of fuels, consisting predominately of carbon and water vapor, and present in sufficient quantity to be seen independently of other matter in the air, such as soil dust and pollens. The discussions in this section focus on smoke from wildland fires, not smoke from the burning of agricultural debris, such as ryegrass residue and fruit tree prunings, or smoke from stoves, fireplaces, and campfires.

Smoke as Air Pollutant

Since smoke from wildfires and prescribed fires can be seen in the atmosphere, it is sometimes considered to be an atmospheric pollutant. However, some scientists wonder if it really is, since it has been a *natural* feature of the environment for thousands of years, just as long as there have been vegetation and fuels to burn. Nothing is more pristine than this type of smoke. Furthermore, smoke from wildland fires will continue to be in the atmosphere on a recurring basis in spite of everything that can be done to prevent it. The paramount question about wildland smoke is: Will it come suddenly in large quantities from intense wildfires of the type discussed in Chapter 3, or will it come more gradually in small amounts from prescribed fires that are set for a good purpose and are managed scientifically? It seems that a solution is the trade-off between wildfires that produce mammoth amounts of smoke and prescribed burning that reduces fire hazards and produces much less smoke.

R. G. Vines, an Australian authority on smoke, has suggested that, since rural smoke has been caused by *natural* forest fires for thousands of years, there is little reason to regard it as a pollutant. As he pointed out in a speech:

We all like the smell of bushfire smoke—and the human race is, we are told, roughly a million years old. If smoke were harmful, it is conceivable that man, from the evolutionary point of view, would have developed some antipathy towards smoke. It is equally conceivable that the highly absorptive carbonaceous components of smoke may serve to keep the earth's atmosphere relatively free of undesirable compounds.

In another speech, Vines said:

Many of the particles in natural smokes consist of finely divided carbon which is highly absorptive. Such carbonaceous components of smoke may have served, in times past, to cleanse the air of undesirable compounds and keep it free of toxic gases (e.g., the sulfurous fumes arising from volcanos). Indeed, bushfire smoke may *still* be beneficial to us all by helping to remove present-day industrial pollutants from the air; and should we, by means of modern technology, ever succeed in preventing the occurrence of rural fires, we might well do ourselves a disservice!

J. Alfred Hall, a chemist and forester, pointed out that about the only penalty inflicted on the environment by prescribed burning is a small and temporary decrease in visibility by particulate matter in the atmosphere. This annoyance, he thought, was a slight penalty for the rewards obtained from prescribed burning to abate a wildfire hazard, and, as we have discovered, to correct other ecological problems associated with attempted fire exclusion.

E. V. Komarek of the Tall Timbers Research Station prepared an excellent ecological review on air pollution from prescribed burning. He emphasized that forest smoke is a component of natural ecosystems; it is not a separate entity, something to be considered by itself. He posed several important questions: (1) Are the carbon particles in the smoke of forest and wildland fires identical with those from people-made sources? (2) Do the artificial carbon particles produced by people have the same absorbing power as those from wildland fires? (3) Are the carbon particles from forest fires one of the basic cleansing mechanisms of the atmosphere? (4) Are the carbon particles from forest fires helping to cleanse the atmosphere of people-made pollution? Komarek's views were shared by V. J. Schaefer, of the Atmospheric Science Research Center at Albany, New York.

Major Emissions from Prescribed Burning

Prescribed fires emit carbon monoxide, carbon dioxide, hydrocarbons, and particulates. Fortunately, only the particulates are of much concern. These are carbon particles, both visible and invisible, caused by incomplete combustion of fuels along with water vapor. The visible portions are what we see and call smoke.

V. J. Schaefer has classified smoke plumes into four categories:

1. The invisible smoke plume. These plumes are produced by very intense fires burning in extremely dry fuels on days of low humidity and windy conditions. In this case, the vapors rising above the fire disappear so quickly that the particles do not aggregate and become large enough to be seen. They are mostly less than 0.1 micron in diameter (the thickness of a human hair is about 100 microns).

In my own research, I have piled dead materials on fires as they burned on dry, windy days, and hardly any visible smoke occurred; only heat waves showed above the fires. This method is one way to limit visible particulates in the atmosphere. Nevertheless, it might not be a good practice because the invisible particles can stay in the atmosphere for a long time, and if smoke is harmful to human health, it could be from these invisible particles entering the aveolar tissue of the lungs. Any coarse particles are well taken care of in the mucociliary system of the respiratory tract.

2. The blue smoke plume. The blue smoke plume comes from a fire that is less intense than the one just described. The particles are mostly 0.15 to 0.3 micron in diameter. The blue color signifies somewhat dry fuels, as well as good meteorological conditions for burning. For the least effect on visibility, this smoke is preferred. This is the kind of smoke I like to see coming from a prescribed fire, especially where the fuels are not heavy.

3. The white smoke plume. This is the type of smoke that one most often sees in understory burning in heavy fuels or wet fuels. Much of the color comes from water vapor. The median size of particles is about 0.6 micron. The smoke is easily seen because this particle size is the most effective of all in producing light-scattering in the visible spectrum.

4. The yellow-grey-black smoke plume. This plume is generally produced by intense wildfires that consume nearly everything in their paths. The yellow and grey colors come from the burning of green materials, and the black comes from burning large volumes of fuels with insufficient ventilation and oxygen supply, as well as from burning fuels high in resin and oil content. This is the type of smoke plume to be avoided in prescribed burning.

Amount of Smoke from Prescribed Fires Versus Wildfires

Studies have shown that prescribed fires produce only about one tenth as much particulate matter per acre of fuels burned as do wildfires. That's because wildfires consume about three times more fuel per acre than prescribed fires, and because the particulate count per ton of fuel consumed is greater. Furthermore, large quantities of green living materials—for example, the foliage of tall trees—may be burned in a wildfire.

Harold Weaver, working in Washington and Arizona, reported that prescribed fires can very effectively reduce fire hazards and limit the acreage burned by wildfires. He said that prescribed burning reduces wildfire incidence by about 78 percent, damage by 87 percent, and cost of control by 55 percent. In Arizona, Harry Kallander found that prescribed burning lessened wildfire size by 60 percent. All of these data suggest that one of the best ways to reduce overall smoke output is through prescribed burning.

Robert Cooper, working in the southeastern United States, made an interesting projection. He estimated that, with no prescribed burning in that area, particulate production from wildfires would be about 3.8 million tons per year. With the present level of prescribed burning, which reduces the acreage of wildfires, the total production is a little over one-half million tons. If the amount of prescribed burning were doubled, reducing still further the occurrence and intensity of wildfires, the particulate matter produced would be only 0.3 million tons. Cooper summarized his findings as follows:

There is no evidence to indicate that air quality has deteriorated more in areas where prescribed fire is used extensively than it has where fire is rarely used. Research information to date (1972) shows that a suspension of prescription burning might actually result in a six-fold annual increase in wildfire acreage in the South. Total particulate production and gaseous emissions from all fires would be about seven times greater without prescribed burning than with it. A little smoke in the right place at the right time may be the best way to avoid the consequences of wildfires and their big smokes.

Factors Affecting Smoke Output

The amount of smoke produced by wildland fires is determined by the quantity of fuels burned, the moisture content of the fuels and the underlying soils, the amount of green living plants consumed, the chemical content of the fuels (for example, the amount of resins and oils), the amount of soil mixed in with the fuels, and the intensity of the fire and its convection.

Factors that tend to create much smoke include the presence of large volumes of fuels (either per acre or by size of the burn), green living vegetation, or ether extractives, or high fire intensity creating much convection. Practices that limit smoke output are burning small volumes of fuels at one time over dry soils, burning when the green plant fraction is at a low level (for example, burning in the understory of conifers before the new grasses make appreciable growth and before poison oak grows new leaves), and burning with low-intensity fires to avoid high convection.

Dispersion of smoke in the atmosphere is another item to be considered. This is determined by meteorological conditions, such as the wind direction and its velocity and persistence, air temperatures at various heights in the atmosphere, and dryness of the air.

Smoke Management

Since smoke output and dispersion are determined by known environmental factors, the burner has an opportunity to regulate these and lessen the nuisance of smoke in sensitive areas such as landscape vistas, airports, towns, and highways. Some of the practices proven effective in smoke management are the following:

1. Start new fires only on "burn days." These are days when meteorological conditions ensure that the smoke will rise up in the atmosphere. Such days are determined by the air pollution control districts and are forecast around four or five o'clock in the afternoon.

2. Burn on days when the smoke plume will be away from smoke-sensitive areas. Weather forecasts are valuable here.

3. Avoid setting fires at night because the smoke can accumulate in patches near the ground, or it may go into cold-air drainageways and cause nuisance problems at lower elevations. It is not always possible to prevent night fires because those already underway may burn continuously for several days. However, one can avoid setting more fires at night.

4. Burn in heavy fuels with short lines of fire. This practice limits the hourly output of smoke. Sometimes the total area to be burned can be limited to a size the fire will cover in one day.

5. Burn under relatively dry fuel conditions. But be careful not to let the fuels become so dry that a prescribed fire can es-

cape control. It would be better to burn when the fuels are a little moist, with more smoke, than to have a fire escape control into heavy fuels and create large quantities of smoke.

6. Burn in the forest understory every two or three years under progressively drier conditions, until the fuels are reduced to a level where the burning can be done rapidly, perhaps by burning upslope, with little smoke production and also under summer dry-fuel conditions.

7. When working in smoke-sensitive areas, pile and burn those portions of the fuels remaining after broadcast burning in the understory of trees, so that very little smoke can go into the atmosphere at any one time.

8. Time the burning to avoid green materials; for example, burn in the understory of trees before green growth becomes advanced.

9. When debris is piled with equipment, avoid mixing in dirt.

10. Do everything possible to avoid fire escapes that might turn into severe wildfires that create much smoke.

11. Persons especially sensitive to smoke should make an effort to stay away from it on days of prescribed burning.

The Clean Air Act

The primary intent and purpose of the Clean Air Act is to protect and enhance the quality of the nation's air resource so as to promote the public health, welfare, and productive capacity. Congress assigned the responsibility of developing what are now known as National Ambient Air Quality Standards to the Environmental Protection Agency (EPA). The states are responsible for attaining and maintaining air quality consistent with standards approved by the EPA. Air pollution control districts are responsible for carrying out the regulations.

When the Clean Air Act was under consideration, Congress focused its attention on motor vehicles and stationary-point emission sources. These, of course, are the two main sources of atmospheric pollutants. I doubt if Congress at that time gave much thought to the smoke coming from prescribed fires.

The Clean Air Act was passed in 1963 and has been amended several times—1966, 1967, 1970, and 1977. Amendments in

1977 emphasized the concept of prevention of significant deterioration of air quality, including visibility. This concept greatly expanded the program for stationary sources of pollution and included, as well, the additional element of visibility protection in Federal Class 1 areas, primarily large national parks and wilderness areas. In this effort, Congress was mainly worried about sources that continuously emit pollutants, not temporary sources, such as prescribed burning. In my opinion, it would be a mistake to regulate out all planned burning in park and wilderness areas. In the long run, that would only lead to more wildfires and more smoke, often at the worst times, and aggravate other environmental problems.

Trade-off of Smoke from Wildfires for That from Prescribed Fires

The idea of trading off the smoke from wildfires for that from prescribed fires is easily explained. Isn't it better to have a little smoke from a prescribed fire than six to ten times more smoke per acre from an uncontrollable wildfire? Furthermore, prescribed fires enhance and protect the environment; wildfires, for the most part, degrade it. In prescribed burning, one has an opportunity to manage the fires and their smoke output and dispersion; in wildfires, there is little or no chance to do this.

Cultural Resources

The term "culture" is used here in the anthropological sense. It includes all the physical evidence—artifacts, structures, and sites—that give some idea of human behavior both in prehistoric, or native, times and in historic, or modern, times. Thus, cultural resources are not limited to the fine arts, such as painting and music, but include all human activity and behavior, such as hunting, cooking, and control burning. Our discussion here is concerned mainly with the effect of prescribed burning on the artifacts and sites of prehistoric times. For a more complete discussion of cultural resources, both prehistoric and historic, I recommend the article "Prescribed Fire Management and Cultural Resource Management" by Peter J.

Pilles, Jr., forest archeologist in Arizona's Coconino National Forest.

With the ever-increasing amount of prescribed burning in wildlands vegetation management, archeologists began to fear that the fires might be doing damage to the prehistoric artifacts' diagnostic features, such as shape, form, weight, and color, on which studies are made. Observations on several wildfire burns had shown that some of the prehistoric ceramic artifacts are severely damaged by the heat of wildfires, but more important was the damage done by bulldozers in scraping firelines, building access roads, and other activities related to fire control. It was logical, then, that archeologists were concerned that the heat of moderate- and low-intensity fires of the type used in prescribed burning might also be doing damage to the diagnostic features of the prehistoric artifacts.

The importance of cultural resources to the American heritage is identified in the National Historic Preservation Act passed by Congress in 1966 and amended in 1980. Among other things, it states that the spirit and direction of the nation are founded on and reflected in its prehistoric and historic heritage, and that these cultural foundations of the nation should be preserved as a living part of our community life and development in order to give a sense of orientation to the American people. Preservation of this irreplaceable heritage is in the public interest so that its vital legacy of cultural, educational, aesthetic, inspirational, economic, and energy benefits will be maintained and enriched for future generations.

The National Historic Preservation Act is administered by the federal agency responsible for lands on which the resources are located. On lands outside of government agencies, provisions are carried out in cooperation with the states, local governments, and firms or individuals. Most land management agencies now have cultural-resource specialists on their staffs.

In response to concerns about damage to cultural resources from prescribed burning, Bruce Kilgore, then associate regional director for resources management for the Western Region of the National Park Service (NPS), in 1978 asked the archeologists and fire ecologists of the NPS to propose jointly a research project addressed to this issue. Observations and studies on wildfire burns were not enough to answer the question, How should the NPS prescribed-burning programs comply with the National Historic Preservation Act, or is there no problem or conflict? According to Roger E. Kelly, regional archeologist in San Francisco, the working hypothesis of the accepted research project was that combustion temperatures from burning debris would alter those valuable diagnostic features of prehistoric artifacts on which archeological research is based. The project included studies on the effects of fire on those nonartifactual materials, such as animal bone and shellfish, found on or in archeological sites, which may also give data on the prehistoric past.

Field research was carried out in different types of fuels in four national park system areas—Yosemite, Sequoia–Kings Canyon, and Grand Canyon national parks and Lava Bed National Monument. At the same time, laboratory research was done at the NPS Western Archeological and Conservation Center at Tucson, Arizona. In the field, 5 by 5–meter plots were established on which artifacts were placed before the burning, photographed, and recovered later. Different amounts of fuels were burned on the plots to test the effects of both high- and moderate-intensity fires and heat duration on the artifacts. Based on these field studies, it was concluded that the burning of duff layers and sparse small-size fuels caused some carbon smudging on the artifacts but did not alter their diagnostic values—namely, surface color, design, integrity and form. Larger fuels, such as logs, which burn longer and with greater intensity of heat, would probably produce adverse effects, but the field tests did not yield sufficient information to prove this assumption.

Meanwhile, in the laboratory at Tucson, Peter Bennett and Michael Kunzmann made a complex series of tests on stone and ceramic artifacts similar to those burned over in the field tests. Their results showed a threshold surface temperature of about 800° F, below which most objects are not changed sufficiently to alter their scientific diagnostic values, but above which water loss, increased friability, discoloration, and change in form did occur. In view of these results, the researchers said in their conclusions and recommendations:

Soil surface temperatures and heating duration found beneath the usual intensity prescription fire do not appear to pose a serious threat to stone or ceramic artifactual materials, provided they are either on or below the soil surface and are small in size. On the other hand, organic materials, such as bone, fiber, and other vegetable matter, may be severely damaged. Each situation requires the use of common sense. The archeologist considering clearance for burning and the re-source manager should bear in mind that the site to be prescription burned has probably been subjected to low-intensity natural fire many times in the past; whatever damage is possible under these con-ditions has already occurred. If the use of high-intensity fire is con-templated (surface temperatures over 400° C [752° F]) or if the site is of high significance, sensitive materials should be removed prior to burning.

Soon after the studies were started, archeologists Patrick Welch of the Bureau of Land Management and Tirzo Gonzales of the Forest Service cooperated with fire ecologists on a project designed to simulate the effects that wildfire and prescribed fire in chaparral have on different types of artifacts. The study was reported by Bill Pidanick, information specialist at the Laguna-Morena Demonstration Area of the Cleveland National Forest in southern California. Two different conditions of chap-arral were selected, one to be burned with a simulated wildfire of high intensity, the other with fire of moderate intensity. Prior to the burning, both prehistoric and historic archeological items were selected and photographed. Some were placed over the soil surface and others at a depth of two inches. The high-intensity fire burned with a flame length up to 20 feet through 38-year-old, 4.5-foot-tall chaparral of chamise and ceanothus. Two weeks earlier, in preparing a site for data collecting, the researchers had placed the cut-off brush over the area to be burned. The fire was set at 11:30 A.M. when the temperature was 84° F, the relative humidity 19 percent, and the wind speed 6 mph. As the fire burned through the chaparral, the soil-surface temperatures reached 800° F, whereas two inches down in the soil they were 102° F. The high-intensity fire caused some damage to about 20 percent of the soil-surface artifacts, while the moderate-intensity fire damaged only 10 percent of them. In both cases, artifacts placed two inches beneath the soil sur-face were undamaged. (See Figure 79.) Pidanick did not report conditions under which the moderate-intensity fire burned.

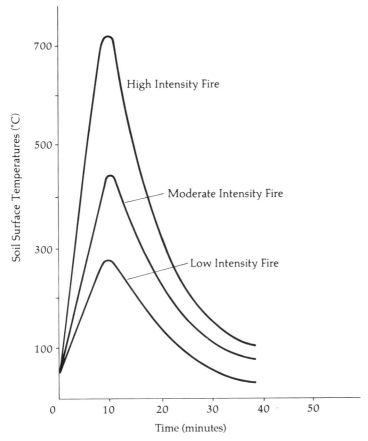

Figure 79. *Soil-surface temperatures during different intensities of burn-ing in southern California chaparral. Soil-surface temperatures below 400°C [752°F], such as prescribed fires produce, do little damage to the archeological resources. (Adapted from research by Leonard Debano and Eugene Conrad.)*

The researchers concluded:

Fire is an inevitable element in the chaparral ecosystem. That we can-not change; we can only postpone it. Over the years we have learned that by postponing this inevitable element, we are faced with the probability of a conflagration-type wildfire which can threaten life and property, destroy watersheds, wildlife, and set the stage for mas-sive mudslides. This type of high-intensity event can cause a great deal of damage to cultural artifacts. Some may even be completely destroyed.

This knowledge of the inevitability of fire, coupled with the data now being compiled through these studies, strongly supports a comprehensive chaparral management program using prescribed fire.

By burning under favorable conditions when the fire intensity is planned and monitored, land managers will be able to proceed with projects in dense chaparral with the knowledge that the obligations for the protection of cultural resources are being met, that cultural artifacts will be impacted to a far lesser degree and most not at all. And the archeologists will be able to do a better field reconnaissance and therefore a better job of documenting archeological sites on National Forest system lands.

In June 1982, Breck Parkman, archeologist for the California Department of Parks and Recreation, inspected a site in William Heise County Park in San Diego County that my students and I had prescribe-burned a few weeks earlier. Following the inspection, he wrote a memorandum to his supervisor, Paul E. Nesbitt, in which he commented:

1. The burn appears to have had no negative external effect upon the pottery at this site. Numerous pot sherds were inspected, with none revealing evidence of damage. What effect the burning might have on scientific testing of these artifacts, such as thermoluminescense, could not be determined from mere external inspection.

2. The burn appears to have had no negative effect upon the chipped stone artifacts and chipping debris at this site. An obsidian flake, several quartz flakes, and a quartz projectile point were inspected, with none revealing evidence of damage of an external nature. What effect the burning might have on scientific testing of these artifacts, such as source analysis of hydration, could not be determined by external inspection.

3. The burn appears to have had no negative external effect on the bedrock milling features at this site. Numerous areas of the bedrock were inspected, with none revealing evidence of external damage. Much of the burned bedrock appeared "sooty," but was washed clean by water.

4. It was not possible to evaluate the burn's effects upon the midden of the site. Refined scientific tests are necessary to evaluate such impact. The one noticeable effect, however, was the addition of char-

coal and ash to the surface of the midden. Percolation through the deposit could contaminate certain scientific tests, such as radiometric dating.

Based on these observations, it appears that prescribed burning in the nearby Cuyamaca Rancho State Park will have little *external* effect on the Park's archeological resources. Just what *internal* effect the burning might have on these resources has yet to be determined. Given the nature of the prescribed burning, it is quite possible that such internal effects would be minimal, if not nonexistent. Until such time as we better understand all the effects that prescribed burning might have on archeological resources, we will be required to follow the management recommendations prepared by Cultural Heritage Planning last year.

Daniel G. Foster, archeologist with the California Department of Forestry and formerly with the California Department of Parks and Recreation, has been recording and evaluating archeological resources for many years. He informed me that in most cases the type of prehistoric resources found in California are not likely to be adversely affected by prescribed burning. Occasionally, however, archeological resources within a proposed burn have been found that require protection—items such as Indian rock art and historic cemeteries with wooden markers.

From the perspective of a cultural resources manager, three things should be done. First, one should find out whether or not the area to be burned has been subjected to fire in the past 75 years or so. If so, most of the perishable items have already been destroyed and further consideration of fire effects is not needed. Second, in all cases, the placement of firelines and their preparation must be considered so that the firelines do not cross archeological sites and construction activities do not disturb them. Without any question, bulldozer scraping can cause a great amount of damage, while hand cleaning will cause the least. Third, if the effects of prescribed burning on prehistoric artifacts and sites are to be carefully evaluated, it is important to have a cultural resources inventory of any area to be burned.

Foster listed as a detrimental effect of prescribed burning the collecting of artifacts by personnel engaged in burning activities and by others just passing through. Especially is this the case where the fire removes vegetation and exposes a site that was previously concealed and not recorded. On the other hand, this exposure could be considered a benefit by a professional archeologist who can properly study the site, prepare site records, and curate the artifacts for future studies.

In summary, research, along with general observations, indicates that prescribed burning with moderate- and low-intensity fires does little or no damage to the diagnostic features of prehistoric artifacts. In those wildland areas burned by wildfires in the past 75 years or so, one can expect that most of the perishable items have already been altered, damaged, or destroyed. One must be careful, however, in preparing firelines and carrying out other activities that might disturb sites. In the few areas that have not burned since fire protection started, perishable items should be protected by firelines or removed.

As far as I know, all government agencies in their prescribed-burning activities are now giving careful attention to the preservation of cultural resources and are fully meeting requirements of the National Historic Preservation Act.

Visual Resource

As wise John Muir said, "Everybody needs beauty as well as bread, places to play in and pray in, where nature may heal and cheer and give strength to body and soul alike." Muir was referring to the giant sequoia groves that we know were molded for centuries by recurring surface fires. What he saw made a lasting impression on him.

The visual resource is the scenery or the view of the landscape. It can be beautiful and inspirational, or it can be ugly and depressing. Its importance to society has grown perceptibly in recent years as more people learn about the health benefits of outdoor recreation and relaxation and about the ill effects of pollutants in the atmosphere, water, and soils. (See Figure 80.)

The importance of the visual resource was recognized in 1969 when the National Environmental Policy Act mandated that the

Figure 80. *A dense Sierran stand of the massive giant sequoias that have thrilled and inspired millions of people. This picture was taken on top of Redwood Mountain in Kings Canyon National Park one year after a prescribed fire that killed the young white fir and removed much debris. Fifty-four trees can be seen from one spot in the general area.*

environment be managed to assure for all Americans safe, beautiful, productive, and aesthetically and culturally pleasing surroundings. The intent of this act was not necessarily to preserve but to put people and nature in productive harmony. This mandate was extended still further in 1976 when the Federal Land Policy and Management Act declared that the public lands administered by the Bureau of Land Management be managed in a manner that will protect the quality of scientific, scenic, historical, ecological, environmental, and archeological values as well as provide commodity resources. Meanwhile, the Endangered Species Act recognized wildlife as an essential component of the visual resource. This act cites the aesthetic, ecological, educational, historical, recreational, and scientific values of endangered species to the nation and its people.

It is interesting to note that all these mandates were preceded by the 1916 National Park Service Organic Act, which declared that the NPS is charged to conserve the scenery and national historic objects and the wildlife therein and to provide enjoyment of them in ways that will leave them unimpaired in future generations. (See Figures 81–85.)

With these mandates in mind, I am listing, first, a few features of the landscape that are largely determined by fire and are beautiful and inspirational and, second, features that may be considered ugly and depressing as a result of fire.

Figure 81. *Three giant sequoias lined up where they started growth—in a trench in which a log had burned, perhaps a century or more ago. As one can see, this area is in need of a prescribed burn to reduce dead fuels and white fir and give new vigor to the giant sequoias.*

Figure 82. *View from a trail in Whitaker's Forest. This area was prescribe-burned, and then cuttings were done to bring the sugar pines in the opening into better view. Now a vista has been created and the sun can shine through onto the pines.*

Pros and Cons of Prescribed Burning

What is it that people like to see in the wildlands? In forested areas, it is a proper ecological balance between young and very old and large trees, open, parklike conditions with vistas, relatively uncluttered ground-cover conditions, and a variety of wildlife species.

Figure 83. *High visual quality in a forest of giant sequoias and mixed conifers in the Mariposa Grove, Yosemite National Park. Here, after a broadcast burn, some cutting was done and then the debris was burned as it was piled. In this case, debris was raked away from the giant sequoias.*

Figure 85. *A giant sequoia (left) in the Placer County Big Tree Grove is becoming lost from view as the dense undergrowth of white fir grows taller. The fire hazard is dangerously high. A prescribed burn followed by some hand-cutting, piling, and burning would greatly improve the visual quality of this grove and at the same time reduce fire hazards to a reasonable level.*

Figure 84. *A giant sequoia with its black, beautifully sculptured fire scar, in the South Grove of Calaveras Big Trees State Park. Since this picture was taken, the area was broadcast-burned and the heavy debris burned in small piles to reduce wildfire hazard.*

Interestingly, all these characteristics were typical of those primitive forests about which early explorers wrote in glowing terms. When these features are lost as a result of fire exclusion, they can be restored and maintained through careful and sensitive use of prescribed fires.

Woodland-savannas are beautiful and the scene is enhanced if livestock are grazing contentedly. In chaparral, it is the mosaics of different age classes of shrubs that most people like to see. Again, these natural conditions can be re-created and maintained by prescribed burning.

The one thing about prescribed burning that some people consider ugly and depressing is the blackening and charring it produces. This can be extensive on some of the trees, particu-

Figure 86. *An area of dense mixed-chaparral, on the Keithly ranch in Lake County, that was burned to improve conditions for wildlife and sheep. Scenes of this sort break the monotony of continuous dense stands and add interest to the landscape. The resulting diversity of age classes of chaparral helps control wildfires and improve conditions for wildlife.*

larly giant sequoia with its fibrous and highly flammable outer bark. Often people are unaware that fire is natural and is necessary for the well-being of the vegetation and the wildlife it supports. (See Figure 86.) Furthermore, the black lasts only a short time, perhaps not more than a few weeks in ponderosa pine, but on incense-cedar, redwood, and giant sequoia it might last for months. In grasslands, the black usually persists from the time of prescribed burning until rains wash the charring down and stimulate a dark green growth of new grasses.

Chapter Seven

Why Not More Prescribed Burning?

Students in fire ecology often ask why more prescribed burning is not being done. Actually, there are many reasons, or excuses. Here are a few.

The Idea That All Fires Are Bad

A prominent German silviculturist who spent several years teaching at the University of California, Berkeley, was asked what he thought of prescribed burning in ponderosa pine. He answered: "In California, with its dry summers and high danger of wildfires, I think prescribed burning might be a good thing. However, I wouldn't be able to do it myself. My early training led me to believe that all forest fires are bad, and when I see charcoal in a forest, it simply rubs me the wrong way." With this point of view, it is certain that this professor did not say much to his students about prescribed burning in forest management. Many professional foresters share his attitude.

Confusing Prescribed Fires with Wildfires

We all know that wildfires in heavy fuels are harmful and costly. Unfortunately, some people do not distinguish these from prescribed fires. Fire is fire, so they think. As an illustration, a well-known forester wanted to find out from me about "all the heresy being taught about fire." It turned out he was talking about summer wildfires. One purpose of prescribed burning, I explained, is to reduce fuels and shape the forests and other wildlands vegetation so that wildfires are not so damaging and are more easily controlled. Our conversation then turned to the difference between prescribed fires and wildfires, and he quickly saw that my "heresy" was to try to *prevent* wildfires.

Too Much Danger of Fires
Escaping Control

A few prescribed fires do escape control. That's because of the extremely high fire hazards that now exist in many wildlands and the lack of properly trained personnel to do the burning. If the personnel are well trained and experienced, the risks of burning are minimal. Furthermore, isn't it more dangerous to live with high fire hazards through periods of low humidity and high winds in the late summer than to burn them out under prescribed conditions? Wouldn't it be better to manage the wildlands in such a way that wildfires could be easily controlled, even in years when the rainfall is below normal?

Too Much Responsibility

Administrators who must approve prescribed-burning plans often fail to do so because of the risks involved. They don't want any responsibility for prescribed burning. Once, for example, just before setting a prescribed fire, the property manager called several of us aside and explained that he was so nervous about the burn that he had not slept for the past two nights. He suggested that we burn in very small units to maintain better control. After a little discussion, though, he allowed us to proceed as we had planned. Obviously, such an administrator and others of similar temperament are not going to encourage prescribed burning. They would rather accept the risk of a wildfire.

Dislike of Smoke from Prescribed Burning

"Too much smoke" is often given as a reason for not control-burning. When I once asked a property manager near Berkeley why he didn't burn under prescription to reduce fire hazards, he answered, "The air pollution control board will not give us a permit." Another property manager when asked the same question, gave exactly the same reply.

These property managers could probably have gotten a permit if the fire chief had said that the burning was planned to abate a severe fire hazard and would be done only on burn days. It is probable that these managers did not want the extra work and responsibility involved in prescribed burning. "Too much smoke" only served as an excuse.

The Public Won't Let Us Burn

Some people think we have to train the general public to accept the idea of prescribed burning. They maintain that people have listened to Smokey the Bear so long that it will be difficult for them to see any benefits from using fire as a tool. But I have found that the general public grasps the ideas very quickly. People often ask, "Why didn't you start it long ago?" The ravages of forest wildfires that we see so often on television are convincing people that something must be done to reduce wildfire hazards if we are to survive in our fire-type environment. My experience has been that it is not difficult to explain this to the general public; on the contrary, it is easy. All we need is more information by television, radio, and other information media.

We Need More Research

The idea that we need more research before any prescribed burning is done seems to be a stalling technique. The fact is that low- and moderate-intensity fires burned through the wildlands vegetation for millions of years, and various elements of the environment had adjusted to them because fire itself was a part of the environment. Of much greater need are studies of the effects of fire exclusion on wildland ecosystems, because keeping fire out introduced a new dimension into the environment.

There Aren't Enough Burn Days

Some fire control officers have said there are only a few days during the year when prescribed burning can be done. Records of the days suitable for burning at Hoberg's were kept from October 1 to April 1 over a four-year period. As many as 47 to 74 days per season proved appropriate. Had the burning continued through April, May, and June, the right days might have been twice that number.

Prescribed Burning Is Too Costly

Those not experienced in burning often give high expense as an excuse for avoiding the practice. The costs and benefits of burning are complex and difficult to assess. Cost depends on the amount of fireline preparation, size of burn, technique of burning, experience of personnel, amount of fuels to be burned, frequency of burning, and so on. I have seen cost figures vary from a few cents to several dollars per acre for broadcast burning. Because of this high variability, it is not wise to write down a specific cost, but if careful planning is done, expense need not be a barrier to burning.

We Can Lose Our Jobs

It has not been many years since some government employees were transferred to other positions if they promoted the idea of prescribed burning. Naturally, this was discouraging to anyone who wanted to be involved in this work. The following three cases illustrate this practice.

Soon after the cattle ranchers began an active program of prescribed burning, a forest ranger wrote an interesting article for the Sunday newspaper praising the burning. The ranger was soon transferred to another position in a town where there was absolutely no chance to be involved in prescribed burning.

In another case, the forest manager wanted to prescribe-burn each year at least as much acreage as the wildfires were burning. Shortly he was transferred to another forest region where there was no opportunity at all for prescribed burning.

The third case is that of a forest manager who wanted to develop a program of rotational burning for chaparral under 30 years of age, almost exactly as I had proposed. Very soon he was transferred to a position in the city, safely away from any involvement in prescribed burning.

There's No Money for Prescribed Burning

A forest manager said he had all the money needed for wildfire suppression but none marked specifically for prescribed burning. He explained that the little money used for prescribed burning came from savings on other projects, and that was why so little prescribed burning was done. Whether his organization had requested funds to be used specifically for prescribed burning was not certain.

Negative Influence of Powerful People

In some cases, management is hindered by opponents of prescribed burning—organizations with money for gifts, and/or individuals with money and time to spend who try to influence people in powerful positions to accept their ideas and work to stop prescribed burning.

Let It Be an Act of God

As a forest ranger and I looked at a brush-covered slope, he remarked that he would never attempt to burn there for fear the fire would escape control. He thought the best thing to do was to leave it alone and let it burn from a lightning-set fire, and then no one could be blamed. This idea is all too prevalent.

In spite of these many reasons, nearly all wildland management agencies have recognized the importance of prescribed fires and have developed programs for burning. Nevertheless, not enough burning is yet being done by any agency. Yosemite and Sequoia–Kings Canyon national parks, for instance, had excellent prescribed-burning programs. In Yosemite, the foresters had planned to burn 14,000 acres per year, but they reduced this to 4,000 acres per year. Reasons for the decline: not enough money for personnel, not enough time, and concern about smoke.

For a prescribed-burning program to progress, more attention must be given to explaining to people, including wildland administrators, what prescribed burning is all about. As I've emphasized throughout this book, people should come to realize that fire is one of the most important features of nature. Prescribed burning is working with nature to accomplish what lightning-set surface fires did for centuries before attempted fire exclusion. Trying to exclude it over long periods, without the use of prescribed fires, leads to terribly destructive wild-

Figure 87. *A highly efficient crew for prescribed burning in ponderosa pine and mixed-conifer forests. We could well afford to have dozens of such crews working to protect our forests from wildfires.*

Berkeley Daily Gazette

An Outstanding Newspaper for an Outstanding Comm

BERKELEY. CALIFORNIA. FRIDAY, SEPTEMBER 17, 1965

60 MPH WINDS RIP BERKELEY

Figure 88. *An ominous headline. To many residents, a dry wind on September 17, 1965, was a strong reminder of the wind on the day of the Berkeley Fire of September 17, 1923. Fortunately, there were no fires on this day in 1965, but fire weather conditions were ripe for another holocaust. One wonders what would have happened if, in some way, three or four fires had been started. Such fire weather conditions are normal for this area, and so the fuels must be reduced to make wildfires easier to control and less destructive.*

fires, horrendous amounts of smoke, and extremely high suppression costs. Uncontrollable wildfires should not be blamed entirely on dry weather and lack of personnel and equipment to fight them, but also on management that allows the fuels to build up beyond all reasonable levels. (See Figures 87–88.) An important step toward having more prescribed burning would be a plan to spend as much money for dealing with those fuels as is spent for other preventative measures and for fire suppression.

If this book helps clarify some of the misunderstandings about prescribed burning and if it stimulates interest in doing such burning to create more ecologically stable conditions in our wildland vegetation, I shall be happy.

Suggested Readings

Introduction

Biswell, H. H. 1959. Man and fire in ponderosa pine in the Sierra Nevada of California. *Sierra Club Bulletin* 44(7):44–53.

———. 1967. Forest fire in perspective. In *Proceedings of the Seventh Annual Tall Timbers Fire Ecology Conference*, 42–66. Tallahassee: Tall Timbers Research Station.

Booysen, Peter de V., and Neil M. Tainton, eds. 1984. *Ecological Effects of Fire in South African Ecosystems.* New York: Springer-Verlag. 426 pp.

Chandler, Craig, et al. 1983. *Fire in Forestry.* Vol. 1, *Forest Fire Behavior and Effects.* New York: Wiley. 450 pp.

Cooper, C. F. 1961. The ecology of fire. *Scientific American* 204(4): 150–160.

Johnston, Verna R. 1970. Fire ecology. In *Sierra Nevada*, 89–118. Boston: Houghton Mifflin.

Kozlowski, T. T., and C. E. Ahlgren, eds. 1974. *Fire and Ecosystems.* New York: Academic Press. 542 pp.

Pyne, Stephen J. 1984. *Introduction to Wildland Fire: Fire Management in the United States.* New York: Wiley. 455 pp.

Wein, Ross, and David M. MacLean, eds. 1984. *The Role of Fire in Northern Circumpolar Ecosystems.* New York: Wiley. 322 pp.

Wright, Henry A., and Arthur W. Bailey. 1982. *Fire Ecology, United States and Southern Canada.* New York: Wiley. 501 pp.

Chapter 1

Albini, Frank A. 1976. Estimating wildfire behavior and effects. USDA Forest Service General Technical Report 30. Ogden, Utah: Intermountain Forest and Range Experiment Station. 92 pp.

Deeming, John E., Robert E. Burgan, and Jack D. Cohen. 1977. The National Fire-Danger Rating System—1977. USDA Forest Service General Technical Report INT-171. Ogden, Utah: Intermountain Forest and Range Experiment Station. 69 pp.

Fischer, William C. 1984. Wilderness fire management planning guide. USDA Forest Service General Technical Report INT-171. Ogden, Utah: Intermountain Forest and Range Experiment Station. 56 pp.

Rothermel, Richard C. 1983. How to predict the behavior of forest and range fires. USDA Forest Service General Technical Report INT-143. Ogden, Utah: Intermountain Forest and Range Experiment Station. 161 pp.

Van Wagtendonk, Jan W. 1974. Refined burning prescriptions for Yosemite National Park. National Park Service Occasional Papers, no. 2. Washington, D.C.: National Park Service. 21 pp.

Chapter 2

Biswell, H. H. 1967. Forest fire in perspective. In *Proceedings of the Seventh Annual Tall Timbers Fire Ecology Conference*, 43–63. Tallahassee: Tall Timbers Research Station.

———. 1975. Placer County Big Tree Grove. *National Parks and Conservation Magazine*, August, pp. 14–17.

Botti, Stephen, and Tom Nichols. 1978. The Yosemite and Sequoia–Kings Canyon prescribed natural fire programs, 1968 to 1978. 13 pp. Mimeograph.

Harvey, H. T., H. S. Shellhammer, and D. E. Stecker. 1980. *Giant Sequoia Ecology, Fire and Reproduction*. Washington, D.C.: U.S. Department of the Interior. 182 pp.

Kilgore, Bruce, and Dan Taylor. 1979. Fire history of a sequoia–mixed conifer forest. *Ecology* 60(1):129–42.

Komarek, E. V. 1967. The nature of lightning fires. In *Proceedings of the Seventh Annual Tall Timbers Fire Ecology Conference*, 5–41. Tallahassee: Tall Timbers Research Station.

Lewis, Henry. 1973. *Patterns of Indian burning in California: Ecology and ethnohistory.* Anthropological Papers, no. 1. Los Altos, Calif.: Ballena Press. 101 pp.

McBride, Joe, and Richard Laven. 1976. Scars as an indicator of fire frequency in the San Bernardino Mountains, California. *Journal of Forestry* 74(7):439–42.

Minnich, Richard A. 1983. Fire mosaics in southern California and northern Baja California. *Bulletin of the American Association for the Advancement of Science* 219:1287–94.

Wagener, Willis. 1961. Past fire incidence in Sierra Nevada forests. *Journal of Forestry* 59(10):739–48.

Chapter 3

Bonnicksen, T. M., and R. G. Lee. 1979. Persistence of a fire exclusion policy in southern California: A biosocial interpretation. *Journal of Environmental Management*, no. 8:277–93.

Countryman, Clive M. 1974. Can southern California wildland conflagrations be stopped? USDA Forest Service General Technical Report PSW-7. Berkeley: Pacific Southwest Forest and Range Experiment Station. 11 pp.

Dodge, Marvin. 1972. Forest fuel accumulation—a growing problem. *Science* 177:139–42.

Holbrook, Stewart. 1943. *Burning an Empire: The Story of American Forest Fires*. New York: Macmillan. 229 pp.

Lee, Myron K. 1977. Marble Cone/Big Sur fire: From the command point of view. *International Fire Chief* 43(9):6–8.

Rogers, Michael J. 1981. Fire management in southern California. In *Proceedings of the Symposium on Dynamics and Management of Mediterranean-Type Ecosystems*, 496–501. USDA Forest Service General Technical Report PSW-58. Berkeley: Pacific Southwest Forest and Range Experiment Station.

Wilson, Carl C. 1970. Commingling of urban and forest fires (a case study of the 1970 California disaster). *Fire Research, Abstracts, and Reviews* 13(1):35–43.

Chapter 4

Agee, James K. 1974. Fire management in the national parks. *Western Wildlands* 1(3):27–33.

Biswell, Harold H. 1980. Fire ecology: Past, present, and future. Speech presented at the American Association for the Advancement of Science conference, Davis, California. 9 pp. Mimeograph.

Botti, Stephen J., and Tom Nichols. 1978. The Yosemite and Sequoia–Kings Canyon prescribed natural fire programs, 1968 to 1978. 13 pp. Mimeograph.

Clar, C. Raymond. 1959. *California Government and Forestry*. Sacramento: California Department of Forestry. 623 pp.

Kilgore, Bruce M. 1976. From fire control to fire management: An ecological basis for policies. In *Transactions of the North American Wild-*

life and Natural Resources Conference, 477–93. Washington, D.C.: Wildlife Management Institute.

Lee, Robert G. 1977. Institutional change in fire management. In *Proceedings of the International Symposium on the Environmental Consequences of Fire and Fuel Management in Mediterranean Ecosystems*, 202–14. USDA Forest Service General Technical Report WO-3. Washington, D.C.: USDA Forest Service.

Moore, William R. 1974. From fire control to fire management. *Western Wildlands* 1(3):11–15.

Schiff, Ashley L. 1962. *Fire and Water—Scientific Hearsay in the Forest Service*. Cambridge: Harvard University Press. 223 pp.

Vogl, Richard J. 1974. Ecologically sound management: Modern man's road to survival. *Western Wildlands* 1(3):6–10.

Chapter 5

Botti, Stephen. 1978. Natural, conditioned, and prescribed fire management plans for Yosemite National Park, Yosemite, Calif. Mimeograph.

Fischer, William C. 1978. Planning and evaluating prescribed fire—A standard procedure. USDA Forest Service General Technical Report INT-43. Ogden, Utah: Intermountain Forest and Range Experiment Station. 19 pp.

Martin, Robert E., and John D. Dell. 1978. Planning for *prescribed burning* in the Inland Northwest. USDA Forest Service General Technical Report PNW-76. Portland, Ore.: Pacific Northwest Forest and Range Experiment Station. 67 pp.

Mobley, H. E., R. S. Jackson, W. E. Balmer, W. E. Ruziska, and W. A. Hough. 1978. *A Guide for Prescribed Fire in Southern Forests*. Atlanta: Southeastern Area, USDA Forest Service. 41 pp.

Van Wagtendonk, Jan W. 1974. Refined burning prescriptions for Yosemite National Park. National Park Service Occasional Papers, no. 2. Washington, D.C.: National Park Service. 21 pp.

Chapter 6

Bendell, J. F. 1974. Effects of fire on birds and mammals. In *Fire and Ecosystems*, edited by T. T. Kozlowski and C. E. Ahlgren, 73–138. New York: Academic Press.

Bennett, Peter S., and Michael Kunzmann. [N.d.] Effects of heat on artifacts: A brief report on work conducted at Western Archeological and Conservation Center, Tucson, Arizona. San Francisco: Western Region, National Park Service. 25 pp. Mimeograph.

Biswell, H. H., and A. M. Schultz. 1957. Surface runoff and erosion as related to prescribed burning. *Journal of Forestry* 55(5):372–74.

———. 1958. Effects of vegetation removal on spring flow. *California Fish and Game* 44(3):211–30.

Biswell, H. H., R. D. Taber, D. W. Hedrick, and A. M. Schultz. 1952. Management of chamise brushlands for game in the north coast region of California. *California Fish and Game* 38:453–84.

Cotton, Lin, and H. H. Biswell. 1973. Forestscape and fire restoration at Whitaker's Forest. *National Parks and Conservation* 47(1):10–15.

Daubenmire, R. 1968. Ecology of fire in grasslands. In *Advances in Ecological Research*, edited by J. B. Cragg, 209–66 (with 212 references). New York: Academic Press.

Hall, J. Alfred. 1972. Forest fuels, prescribed fire and air quality. Portland, Ore.: Pacific Northwest Forest and Range Experiment Station. 44 pp.

Kelley, Roger E. 1981. Tentative results of research regarding fire impacts upon archeological resources. San Francisco: Western Region, National Park Service. 6 pp. Mimeograph.

Kilgore, Bruce M. 1971. Response of breeding birds to habitat change in giant sequoia forests. *American Midland Naturalist* 85(1):135–52.

Komarek, E. V., Sr. 1970. Controlled burning and air pollution: An ecological review. In *Proceedings of the Tenth Tall Timbers Fire Ecology Conference*, 141–73. Tallahassee: Tall Timbers Research Station.

Lawrence, George. 1966. Ecology of vertebrate animals in relation to chaparral fire in the Sierra Nevada foothills. *Ecology* 47(2):278–90.

Longhurst, William M. 1978. Responses of bird and mammal population to fire in chaparral. *California Agriculture* (October):9–12.

Lyon, L. Jack, H. S. Crawford, Eugene Czuhai, R. L. Fredericksen, R. F. Harlow, L. J. Metz, and H. A. Pearson. 1978. Effects of fire on fauna: A state-of-knowledge review. USDA Forest Service General Technical Report WO-6. Washington, D.C.: USDA Forest Service. 41 pp.

McIlridge, William A. 1984. An assessment of the effects of prescribed burning on soil erosion in chaparral. Davis, Calif.: USDA Soil Conservation Service. 102 pp.

Mayfield, Harold F. 1978. Brood parasitism: Reducing interactions between Kirtland's warblers and brown-headed cowbirds. In *Endangered Birds: Management Techniques for Preserving Threatened Species*, edited by Stanley A. Temple, 85–91. Madison: University of Wisconsin Press.

———. 1987. Bird of fire: Kirtland's warbler update. *Michigan Audubon News* 35 (May–June):8–9.

National Academy of Sciences. 1976. *Air Quality and Smoke from Urban and Forest Fires: Proceedings of International Symposium.* Washington, D.C. 381 pp.

Nichols, R., T. Adams, and J. Menke. 1984. Shrubland management for livestock forage. In *Shrublands in California: Literature Review and Research Needed for Management,* edited by Johannes J. Devries, 104–21 (with 74 references). Davis: Water Resources Center, University of California.

Pidanick, Bill. 1982. Prescribed fire/cultural artifacts: Investigating the effects. San Diego: Cleveland National Forest. 5 pp. Mimeograph.

Pilles, Peter J., Jr. 1982. Prescribed fire management and cultural resource management. Flagstaff, Ariz.: Coconino National Forest, USDA Forest Service. 10 pp. Mimeograph.

Task Force on Clean Air Act Regulations. 1980. Wildland fires, air quality, and smoke management. *Journal of Forestry* 78(11):689–97.

Turner, Kenneth M. 1985. Water salvage through vegetation management in California. Sacramento: California Department of Water Resources. 12 pp. Mimeograph.

U.S. Forest Service. 1979. *Proceedings of the Workshop in Visibility Values.* USFS General Technical Report WO-18. Washington, D.C.: USDA Forest Service. 153 pp.

Vogl, Richard J. 1974. Effects of fire in grasslands. In *Fire and Ecosystems,* edited by T. T. Kozlowski and C. E. Ahlgren, 139–94 (with 284 references). New York: Academic Press.

Welch, Pat, and Tirzo Gonzales. 1982. Research design: Prescribed burn impact evaluation upon cultural resources, LMDA and Thing Mountain chaparral management projects. San Diego: Cleveland National Forest. 8 pp. Mimeograph.

Wright, Henry A., and Arthur W. Bailey. 1982. *Fire Ecology, United States and Southern Canada.* New York: Wiley. 501 pp.

Index

Compositor: G&S Typesetters
Text: 11/13 Palatino
Display: Palatino
Printer: Malloy Lithographing, Inc.
Binder: Malloy Lithographing, Inc.